The Law Commission
Consultation Paper No 193

SIMPLIFICATION OF CRIMINAL LAW: PUBLIC NUISANCE AND OUTRAGING PUBLIC DECENCY

A Consultation Paper

ISBN: 9780118404747

Printed in the UK for The Stationery Office Limited
on behalf of the Controller of Her Majesty's Stationery Office

ID P002356680 03/10

Printed on paper containing 75% recycled fibre content minimum.

THE LAW COMMISSION – HOW WE CONSULT

About the Law Commission
The Law Commission was set up by section 1 of the Law Commissions Act 1965 for the purpose of promoting the reform of the law.

The Law Commissioners are: The Rt Hon Lord Justice Munby (*Chairman*), Professor Elizabeth Cooke, Mr David Hertzell, Professor Jeremy Horder and Miss Frances Patterson QC. The Chief Executive is: Mr Mark Ormerod.

Address for correspondence: Steel House, 11 Tothill Street, London SW1H 9LJ.

Topic of this consultation
This consultation paper deals with the offences of public nuisance and outraging public decency. A summary of the main points can be found in paras 1.11 to 1.16.

Scope of this consultation
The purpose of this consultation is to generate responses to our provisional proposals.

Geographical scope
The contents of this consultation paper refer to the law of England and Wales.

Impact assessment
An impact assessment is included.

Duration of the consultation
We invite responses from 31 March 2010 to 30 June 2010.

How to respond
Send your responses either –

By email to: public.nuisance@lawcommission.gsi.gov.uk   OR

By post to: Simon Tabbush at the address above

Tel: 020-3334 0273 / Fax: 020-3334 0201

If you send your comments by post, it would be helpful if, whenever possible, you could send them to us electronically as well (for example, on CD or by email to the above address, in any commonly used format).

After the consultation
In the light of the responses we receive, we will decide our final recommendations and we will present them to Parliament. We hope to publish our report by November 2011. It will be for Parliament to decide whether to approve any changes to the law.

Code of Practice
We are a signatory to the Government's Code of Practice on Consultation and carry out our consultations in accordance with the Code criteria (set out on the next page).

Freedom of information
We will treat all responses as public documents in accordance with the Freedom of Information Act and we may attribute comments and include a list of all respondents' names in any final report we publish. If you wish to submit a confidential response, you should contact us before sending the response. PLEASE NOTE – We will disregard automatic confidentiality statements generated by an IT system.

Availability of this consultation paper
You can view/download it free of charge on our website at: **http://www.lawcom.gov.uk/docs/cp193.pdf**.

CODE OF PRACTICE ON CONSULTATION

o **THE SEVEN CONSULTATION CRITERIA**

Criterion 1: When to consult

Formal consultation should take place at a stage when there is scope to influence the policy outcome.

Criterion 2: Duration of consultation exercise

Consultations should normally last for at least 12 weeks with consideration given to longer timescales where feasible and sensible

Criterion 3: Clarity and scope of impact

Consultation documents should be clear about the consultation process, what is being proposed, the scope to influence and the expected costs and benefits of the proposals.

Criterion 4: Accessibility of consultation exercises

Consultation exercises should be designed to be accessible to, and clearly targeted at, those people the exercise is intended to reach.

Criterion 5: The burden of consultation

Keeping the burden of consultation to a minimum is essential if consultations are to be effective and if consultees' buy-in to the process is to be obtained.

Criterion 6: Responsiveness of consultation exercises

Consultation responses should be analysed carefully and clear feedback should be provided to participants following the consultation.

Criterion 7: Capacity to consult

Officials running consultations should seek guidance in how to run an effective consultation exercise and share what they have learned from the experience.

o **CONSULTATION CO-ORDINATOR**

The Law Commission's Consultation Co-ordinator is Phil Hodgson.

o You are invited to send comments to the Consultation Co-ordinator about the extent to which the criteria have been observed and any ways of improving the consultation process.

o **Contact:** Correna Callender, Consultation Co-ordinator, Law Commission, Steel House, 11 Tothill Street, London SW1H 9LJ – Email: correna.callender@lawcommission.gsi.gov.uk

100611 7789

Full details of the Government's Code of Practice on Consultation are available on the BERR website at http://www.berr.gov.uk/files/file47158.pdf.

THE LAW COMMISSION

SIMPLIFICATION OF CRIMINAL LAW: PUBLIC NUISANCE AND OUTRAGING PUBLIC DECENCY

CONTENTS

PART 1: INTRODUCTION — 1

The general aim of the simplification project — 1.3 — 1

The current project: public nuisance and outraging public decency — 1.11 — 2

PART 2: PUBLIC NUISANCE: EXISTING LAW AND PRACTICE — 5

The issues in brief — 2.1 — 5

The law in more detail — 2.7 — 7

    The act or omission — 2.9 — 7

    The effect — 2.19 — 11

    The fault element — 2.36 — 16

Current practice — 2.46 — 19

Alternatives to public nuisance — 2.52 — 20

    Environmental nuisance — 2.53 — 20

    Behavioural nuisance — 2.59 — 23

Other countries — 2.61 — 25

PART 3: OUTRAGING PUBLIC DECENCY: THE EXISTING LAW — 28

    Conduct element: the activities covered — 3.2 — 28

    Circumstance and consequence elements — 3.16 — 34

    Fault element — 3.39 — 41

Other countries — 3.43 — 42

    Australia — 3.43 — 42

    Canada — 3.44 — 43

    New Zealand — 3.46 — 44

PART 4: CRITICISMS AND PROPOSALS: THE CONDUCT ELEMENT — 46

Public nuisance — 4.1 — 46

    Abolishing the offence — 4.1 — 46

    Reforming the conduct element — 4.24 — 52

Outraging public decency — 4.28 — 52

    Abolishing the offence — 4.28 — 52

    Reforming the conduct element — 4.37 — 54

    Provisional proposal — 4.42 — 55

PART 5: CRITICISMS AND PROPOSALS: THE FAULT ELEMENT   57

Offences in general and fault requirements	5.2	57
Particular offences with similar fault elements	5.9	59
Some analogous offences	5.9	59
How the offences cover similar ground	5.14	60
The fault element in the analogous offences: strict and constructive liability	5.22	61
Public nuisance	5.32	63
Outraging public decency	5.45	66

PART 6: RESTATING THE OFFENCES IN STATUTE   69

Public nuisance	6.1	69
Provisional proposal	6.8	70
Sentencing	6.10	70
Outraging public decency	6.12	71
Provisional proposals	6.15	71
Sentencing	6.16	72

PART 7: PROVISIONAL PROPOSALS AND QUESTIONS FOR CONSULTATION   73

Public nuisance	7.1	73
Outraging public decency	7.5	73
Additional questions for consultation	7.8	74

APPENDIX A: IMPACT ASSESSMENT FOR REFORMING THE OFFENCES OF PUBLIC NUISANCE AND OUTRAGING PUBLIC DECENCY   75

PART 1
INTRODUCTION

1.1 The Law Commission has embarked on a new programme of 'simplification' of the criminal law, including criminal evidence and procedure.[1] Simplification involves:

(1) giving the law a clearer structure;

(2) using more modern terminology;

(3) making the law in a given area more consistent with other closely allied areas of law;

(4) making the law readily comprehensible to ordinary people by ensuring that it embodies sound and sensible concepts of fairness.

1.2 It is envisaged that the simplification project will take the form of a rolling programme reviewing several areas of the criminal law in turn. The present review of public nuisance and outraging public decency is the first instalment of that project.[2]

THE GENERAL AIM OF THE SIMPLIFICATION PROJECT

1.3 Simplification is not the same as codification, although the former can be done with a view to making the latter easier. As explained in the Tenth Programme:

> The Commission continues to support the objective of codifying the law, and will continue to codify where it can, but considers that it needs to redefine its approach to make codification more achievable. This project is an important component of that redefinition. We believe that simplification of the criminal law is a necessary step in furtherance of its codification.

1.4 Simplification will commonly be aimed at making only relatively modest legal changes. It may involve recommending the abolition of an offence, as discussed in the relevant paragraphs of the Tenth Programme, if it has become redundant. Alternatively it may recommend that a common law offence be restated in statutory form, thus achieving partial codification. Otherwise, it will be concerned with removing clear injustices or anomalies.

1.5 This project will be concerned, in the first instance, with placing a range of common law crimes in statutory form or, if those crimes have become redundant, with recommending their abolition.

1.6 The project will not be concerned with the common law crimes of murder, manslaughter and conspiracy to defraud. Changes to such offences cannot be recommended solely in the name of 'simplification', because the numerous

---

[1] Tenth Programme of Law Reform (Law Com No 311), para 2.24 and following.

[2] Tenth Programme, para 2.32.

issues of public policy at stake make reform a matter best tackled through the normal wide-ranging process of CP and report.

1.7 As a part of each CP and report on simplification, it may be necessary or desirable to recommend changes to statutory crimes in the same or in an allied area of law, with a view to making the law both fairer and better suited to ultimate codification.

1.8 As the project develops, it may be extended to encompass crimes already in statutory form that are in need of modernisation, merger with other offences, abolition or reform. However, there will still be a distinction between the statutory crimes considered as part of the simplification project and Law Commission work on other areas of the criminal law. The simplification project will not be concerned with reforms which can only be recommended following consultation on large or difficult policy questions.

1.9 The areas of common law that have been selected for consideration in the first instance are as follows. The first two are mentioned in the Tenth Programme.

(1) Public nuisance and outraging public decency.

(2) False imprisonment and kidnapping.

(3) Offences against the administration of justice and the public interest, including:

(a) refusal to serve in a public office;

(b) failure by a common innkeeper to provide board and lodging;

(c) escape, breach of prison and rescue from lawful custody.

1.10 In spite of the fact that a simplification project has quite modest aims, it would not be undertaken unless there was a strong reason for changing the law in the way recommended. We believe that there will almost always be such a reason to introduce a simplified law that is not only clearer and easier for judges to explain and (where relevant) for juries to understand, but also more consistent with overlapping areas of law and fairer by targeting only blameworthy behaviour.

THE CURRENT PROJECT: PUBLIC NUISANCE AND OUTRAGING PUBLIC DECENCY

1.11 This initial simplification project is concerned with the common law offences of public nuisance and of outraging public decency.

1.12 The term "public nuisance" has historically been used in two senses. In a narrow sense, it referred to activities which affect the safety or amenity of an area. In a wide sense it referred to a family of public order offences, including public nuisance proper, outraging public decency and keeping a disorderly house, and several offences now abolished such as being a nightwalker or a common scold. In recent years the tendency has been to confine public nuisance more closely around the environmental category of activities and to treat outraging public decency and keeping a disorderly house as separate offences.[3]   All these offences were developed by the King's Bench in the seventeenth and eighteenth centuries in reaction to perceived social evils, though public nuisance proper also has older roots. They had in common a vagueness of outline and a reluctance to define a fault element, as the purpose was to remove the nuisance rather than to reform the offender.

1.13   Given the review of sexual offences resulting in the Sexual Offences Act 2003 we do not propose to consider the offence of keeping a disorderly house. The existing law and practice on public nuisance, including an account of overlapping statutory offences and the law in some other countries, are discussed in Part 2. The existing law on outraging public decency is discussed in Part 3.

1.14   For both offences, we treat the following questions in order.

(1)   Whether the offence is still necessary.

(2)   Whether the factual ingredients of the offence should be revised, or are now sufficiently consolidated by case law so as not to need further reform.

We discuss both these issues in Part 4.

(3)   Whether the fault element should be strengthened to require intention or recklessness, in line with more usual criminal offences.

We discuss this issue in Part 5.

(4)   Whether it is desirable in principle, and opportune at present, to restate the offence in statutory form.

We discuss this issue in Part 6.

1.15   The proposal, for public nuisance and outraging public decency, is to require the prosecution to prove that the defendant intended a public nuisance or outrage to public decency to occur, or was reckless as to whether his or her conduct would amount to or cause such an occurrence. We also consider that both offences should be restated in statutory form.

1.16   We believe that these changes would:

(1)   make the law fairer to accused persons and more certain in giving fair warning of when criminal liability may be incurred;

(2)   bring the law into line, so far as the fault element is concerned, with crimes of comparable gravity that may cover the same ground, such as criminal damage or offences against public order;

---

[3]   For more detail see paras 2.11-2.12 below.

(3)   improve the clarity of the law by employing fault elements with a now well-understood legal meaning.

PART 2
PUBLIC NUISANCE: EXISTING LAW AND PRACTICE

THE ISSUES IN BRIEF

2.1   A traditional definition of public nuisance is given in the 2010 edition of Archbold's *Criminal Pleading, Evidence and Practice* (henceforth "*Archbold*").[1]

> A person is guilty of a public nuisance (also known as common nuisance), who (a) does an act not warranted by law, or (b) omits to discharge a legal duty, if the effect of the act or omission is to endanger the life, health, property or comfort of the public, or to obstruct the public in the exercise or enjoyment of rights common to all Her Majesty's subjects.

This definition is approved in *Rimmington and Goldstein*, the leading modern case on the subject.[2]   We discuss the source of the wording below.[3]

2.2   Examples of public nuisance are:

   (1)   obstructing the highway;[4]

   (2)   blasting and quarrying near built-up areas;[5]

   (3)   allowing land to be used as a dump, creating a dangerous or noxious environment;[6]

   (4)   noisy parties and "raves";[7]

   (5)   bomb hoaxes and false calls to the emergency services;[8]

   (6)   hanging from motorways and bridges, for example in political demonstrations;[9]

   (7)   keeping pumas in a domestic garden;[10]

   (8)   gang activity involving drug dealing in an urban area.[11]

---

[1]   Para 31-40.

[2]   [2006] 1 AC 459 (HL), discussed para 2.17 below.

[3]   Paras 2.7, 2.8 and 2.19.

[4]   *Dymond v Pearce* [1972] 1 QB 496.

[5]   *Attorney-General v PYA Quarries* [1957] 2 QB 169.

[6]   *Attorney-General v Tod Heatley* [1897] 1 Ch 560.

[7]   *Shorrock* [1994] QB 279.

[8]   *Madden* [1975] 1 WLR 1379.

[9]   Information supplied by Crown Prosecution Service.

[10]   *Wheeler, The Times* 17 December 1971.

2.3 The legal effect of a public nuisance is threefold.

    (1)   If someone is affected to an exceptional degree, distinguishable from the effect on the general or local public, the person affected can sue in tort.

    (2)   If the person responsible knew, or ought to have known, of the bad effects on the public, he or she is guilty of a criminal offence.

    (3)   The Attorney General, the local authority or the person affected may bring proceedings for an injunction.

2.4 We argue below[12] that the tort is the fundamental part of public nuisance, and that both the offence and the injunction procedure are outgrowths of it.[13] Be that as it may, the majority of cases defining what a public nuisance is are tort cases, but these definitions are equally applicable to the offence.[14]

2.5 The offence has been extensively criticised in an article by J R Spencer.[15] His first argument is that the offence is so wide and the definition is so fluid that it lacks the certainty required of a criminal offence. His second argument is that almost all examples of public nuisance are now covered by specialised statutory offences. He concludes that the offence should be abolished, either without replacement or in favour of a narrower offence of doing anything which creates a major hazard to the physical safety or health of the public.[16]

2.6 Since then, the offence of public nuisance has been restated and reconsidered by the House of Lords in *R v Rimmington and Goldstein*.[17] These were two appeals raising separate issues.

    (1)   *Rimmington* concerned a person who engaged in a campaign of sending racially abusive hate mail. It was held that this did not fall within the offence, which only addressed acts or omissions which injured the public collectively and not series of acts against individuals.

    (2)   *Goldstein* concerned a person who put salt into a letter as a joke, thus causing an anthrax scare and disrupting the sorting office. It was held that the defendant did not satisfy the fault element of the offence, which

---

[11] The significance of this last example is not that the dealers are prosecuted for public nuisance (there are more appropriate offences) but that injunctions can be granted: *Nottingham City Council v Zain* [2001] EWCA Civ 1248, [2002] 1 WLR 607.

[12] Para 5.41.

[13] Simester and Sullivan, *Criminal Law: Theory and Doctrine* (2nd edition) pp 243-4 points out that some features of the tort, such as vicarious liability, also apply to the crime and that in some respects the offence has more affinity with the law of tort than the law of crime.

[14] Blackstone's Commentaries iv 167, in defining the offence of public nuisance, refers back to the discussion of the tort before going on to give further examples. *Rimmington*, discussed below, refers to *PYA Quarries*, which was a civil case, as "the leading modern authority on public nuisance": para 18.

[15] "Public Nuisance — a critical examination" [1989] CLJ 55 (hereinafter "Spencer").

[16] Spencer, pp 83-84.

[17] [2006] 1 AC 459 (HL).

required that he should reasonably have foreseen the consequences of his actions.

THE LAW IN MORE DETAIL

2.7 The source of the wording in the *Archbold* definition given above[18] appears to be Sir James Stephen's *A Digest of the Criminal Law*, where public (or common) nuisance is defined as:

> an act not warranted by law or an omission to discharge a legal duty, which act or omission obstructs or causes inconvenience or damage to the public in the exercise of rights common to all Her Majesty's subjects.

2.8 Similar contemporary definitions are quoted in *Rimmington*,[19] and wording based on Stephen's has been used in the criminal codes of some Commonwealth countries.[20] We consider below[21] some of the differences between the various formulations.

The act or omission

2.9 The first part of the definition, concerning acts not warranted by law or omissions to discharge a legal duty, is problematic. On one interpretation, "acts not warranted by law" could be confined to unlawful acts in the sense of identifiable offences.[22] At the other extreme, it could mean any act that has the relevant effect of public harm and is not covered by specific statutory authority. Similarly it is not clear whether a "legal duty" means a specific duty imposed on a person in the defendant's position (e.g. as a public functionary, employer or landowner) or extends to a common law duty of care or indeed the duty of reasonable use of land as known to the law of private nuisance. In a very broad way it is clear what these definitions are aiming at: anyone doing something that obviously and severely affects the safety or comfort of the neighbourhood has the burden of justifying it.

2.10 A possible explanation for this may be found in Spencer's analysis of the history of the offence. According to him, public nuisance was not originally the name of an offence, but rather a generic description of the power of the court to create offences in response to public disorder.[23] This was compounded by the legislative practice of creating new offences and declaring them to be forms of public nuisance,[24] and by the tendency of legal writers such as Hawkins[25] to list miscellaneous public order offences under "public nuisance" for convenience of

---

[18] Para 2.1.

[19] Lord Bingham's speech, para 10.

[20] *Rimmington*, paras 10 and 11, and para 2.61 and following, below.

[21] Para 2.19.

[22] This narrow meaning is the one accepted in Canada, where however the statutory phrase is "unlawful act" rather than "act not warranted by law": para 2.66 below.

[23] Spencer, pp 61 to 63. He makes a similar point in relation to Hawkins' definition: pp 65-66.

[24] Spencer, pp 63 to 64.

[25] *Pleas of the Crown* (1716).

classification.[26]   In that sense, public nuisance does indeed include, at least potentially, every "act not warranted by law" that has adverse public effects.

2.11   While there is some truth in this, it appears to us to underrate the importance of the core cases where there is a clear analogy with private nuisance. Accordingly, we may divide historical instances of public nuisance into two categories.

(1)   The first category, of nuisance proper, consists of those cases where there is a clear analogy with private nuisance. In private nuisance, the claimant must demonstrate damage to himself or herself in the enjoyment of immoveable property, whether in the form of land or of an incorporeal right such as a right of way. Similarly in a public nuisance properly so called there must be detriment either to the neighbourhood generally or to a public right such as a highway.

(2)   The second category consists of all the public mischiefs described together with nuisance proper by the legal classics, such as Foster, Hawkins and Blackstone. These included examples like keeping a disorderly house and being a nightwalker or a common scold. Some of the examples given by the classical writers are offences created by statute, while even the common law examples are arguably separate offences, classified with nuisance proper only for convenience of exposition. In some cases there may be an overlap, as keeping a disorderly house may well depress property prices or impair the amenities of the area, but it would strain language to justify all instances of public nuisance in this way. In summary, nuisances within the second category cannot be defined comprehensively by a single verbal formula, but only piecemeal, by a test of similarity to the particular nuisances that have been found in the past.

2.12   As *Rimmington* excludes series of acts aimed at individuals from the scope of the offence, the second category, as described above, is clearly not as fluid or as extensive as it was.[27] Of the older historical instances, most either have been abolished without replacement[28] or are now covered by statutory offences. Two common law instances continue to exist, but are no longer considered to be forms of public nuisance.

(1)   The offence of keeping a disorderly house still exists, but the conditions for being a public nuisance need not be met.[29]

(2)   Similarly there is still an offence of outraging public decency.[30]

2.13   The definition, in speaking of "an act not warranted by law", suggests that a single act is sufficient.[31]   This appears from the case of *Ong*,[32] where the

---

[26]   Spencer, p 65.

[27]   Para 2.27 below.

[28]   Criminal Law Act 1967 s 13 abolishes the offences of eavesdropping or being a common barrator, a common scold or a common night walker.

[29]   *Quinn, Bloom* [1962] 2 QB 245.

[30]   *Hamilton* [2007] EWCA Crim 2062, [2008] QB 224; leave to appeal refused [2008] 1 WLR 425. We discuss this offence in Part 3 below.

defendant conspired to switch off the floodlights at a Premiership football match so as to cause the match to be abandoned, though the issue was not argued as it was a sentencing appeal. Earlier, Denning LJ in *A-G v PYA Quarries*[33] had also held that a single act was sufficient, and that this was one distinction between public and private nuisance. This case involved quarrying activities which inconvenienced the neighbours by noise, vibration and falling dust and rocks.

> I quite agree that a private nuisance always involves some degree of repetition or continuance. An isolated act which is over and done with, once and for all, may give rise to an action for negligence or an action under the rule in *Rylands v Fletcher*,[34] but not an action for nuisance. A good example is an explosion in a factory which breaks windows for miles around. It gives rise to an action under *Rylands v Fletcher*, but no other action if there was no negligence: see *Read v J Lyons & Co.*[35] But an isolated act may amount to a public nuisance if it is done under such circumstances that the public right to condemn it should be vindicated. I referred to some authorities on this point in *Southport Corporation v Esso Petroleum Co.*[36] In the present case, in view of the long history of stones, vibrations and dust, I should think it incumbent on the defendants to see that nothing of the kind happens again such as to be injurious to the neighbourhood at large, even on an isolated occasion.

2.14   As the facts in *PYA Quarries* involved continuing acts of blasting, the observation about an isolated act was not necessary to the decision and therefore not a binding precedent. Denning LJ, having held that the facts of the case inconvenienced enough people to be regarded as public rather than private nuisance, proceeded to consider the remaining differences between the two. Smith and Hogan's *Criminal Law* (henceforth "*Smith and Hogan*") also casts doubt on this distinction, saying that "the House of Lords rejected that interpretation of the offence in *Rimmington*".[37]

2.15   The relevant paragraph in *Rimmington*, as set out in full below,[38] does not in fact address the distinction between an isolated and a continuing act. If *Rimmington* is inconsistent with Denning LJ's dictum in *PYA Quarries*, it is by clarifying that an act is not a public nuisance only because "it is done under such circumstances that the public right to condemn it should be vindicated". So far as the question of one act or many is concerned, the effect is almost the opposite of what *Smith*

---

[31]   There may be a requirement that the act should have continuing effects, but that is a separate issue: para 2.35 below.

[32]   [2001] 1 Cr App Rep (S) 404.

[33]   [1957] 2 QB 169, 192.

[34]   (1868) LR 3 HL 330. The rule in question establishes strict liability for the escape of anything kept on land which would not be there as part of the normal use of that land.

[35]   [1947] AC 156.

[36]   [1954] 2 QB 182, 197.

[37]   *Smith and Hogan* 12th edition para 32.2.1.3 (p 1091), citing *Rimmington* para 37. In this paper, all references to "Smith and Hogan" are to the 12th edition unless otherwise stated.

[38]   Para 2.27 below.

and Hogan appears to suggest. The facts of *Rimmington*, like those of the cases which it overrules, are excluded from the offence not because they involved a single act but because they involved a continuing series of acts each of which only affected one individual. We return to this point below.[39]

2.16   Public nuisance can also be perpetrated by omission. An example is allowing a house to fall into ruin[40] or allowing one's land to be used as a rubbish tip.[41] Again the omission must have a sufficiently deleterious effect on the public, but there does not appear to be a requirement that the omission must constitute a legal wrong separate from nuisance (except that, if the effect is reasonably foreseeable, the omission arguably amounts to the tort of negligence).

2.17   *Rimmington* does not specifically discuss the first part of the definitions, concerning acts not warranted by law and omission to discharge a legal duty. However, after discussing the requirements of certainty in criminal offences,[42] Lord Bingham goes on to say:[43]

> I would for my part accept that the offence as defined by Stephen, as defined in *Archbold* (save for the reference to morals), as enacted in the Commonwealth codes quoted above and as applied in the cases … referred to in paras 13 to 22 above is clear, precise, adequately defined and based on a discernible rational principle. A legal adviser asked to give his opinion in advance would ascertain whether the act or omission contemplated was likely to inflict significant injury on a substantial section of the public exercising their ordinary rights as such: if so, an obvious risk of causing a public nuisance would be apparent; if not, not.

In this, he implicitly adopts the definitions. Lord Rodger does the same.[44]

2.18   The gist of the above passage in *Rimmington*, and of the passage about the "requirement of common injury",[45] is that it is on that requirement, as embodied in the second half of the definition, that public nuisance turns. The implication is that the first half of the definition is not a significant limitation and that if there is a doubt about its meaning it should be interpreted in the widest sense. That is, any act which brings about the relevant common injury is unlawful unless there is specific legal authority for it, and any omission to do what one is reasonably expected to do to prevent the relevant common injury is a breach of a legal duty of care. This is borne out by cases such as *PYA Quarries*: quarrying and blasting are not, in themselves and apart from the common injury caused, unlawful acts.

---

[39]   Paras 2.25 to 2.28.

[40]   *Watts* (1703) 1 Salk 357, 91 ER 311.

[41]   *A-G v Tod Heatley* [1897] 1 Ch 560.

[42]   Para 4.8 below and following.

[43]   *Rimmington*, para 36.

[44]   *Rimmington*, para 45.

[45]   *Rimmington*, para 10.

The effect

2.19 The second half of the definition concerns the effect on the public. A variety of formulations is quoted in *Rimmington*.[46] Examples are:

> … which causes any common injury, danger or annoyance to the public or to the people in general who dwell or occupy property in the vicinity, or which must necessarily cause injury, obstruction, danger or annoyance to persons who may have occasion to use any public right.[47]

> … which act or omission endangers the lives safety health property or comfort of the public, or by which the public are obstructed in the exercise or enjoyment of any right common to all Her Majesty's subjects.[48]

> … which act or omission obstructs or causes inconvenience or damage to the public in the exercise of rights common to all Her Majesty's subjects.[49]

> … if the effect of the act or omission is to endanger the life, health, property, morals, or comfort of the public, or to obstruct the public in the exercise or enjoyment of rights common to all Her Majesty's subjects.[50]

These are generically referred to in *Rimmington* as the "requirement of common injury", which is "a, perhaps *the*, distinguishing feature of this offence".[51]

2.20 The requirement of common injury gives rise to four questions:

(1) injury to whom (or to how many)?

(2) what type of injury?

(3) how great an injury?

(4) for how long?

Injury to whom?

2.21 Some of the older definitions appear to suggest that a public nuisance must be an annoyance to "all the King's subjects".[52] *Smith and Hogan* points out[53] that, taken literally, this is an absurdity.[54]

---

[46] Paras 8 to 11.

[47] Indian Penal Code 1860, s 268.

[48] Draft Criminal Code of 1879, s 150.

[49] Stephen, para 2.7 above.

[50] Archbold, *Criminal Pleading, Evidence and Practice* (2005 edition) para 31–40.

[51] *Rimmington*, para 10.

[52] E.g. Blackstone's Commentaries iii 216.

2.22   One kind of public nuisance, and in a way the classical instance, is the obstruction of a public highway. Here the analogy with private nuisance is clear: to obstruct a private right of way is an injury to the owner of that right, so to obstruct a public right of way is an injury to the public at large. The point here is not that all members of the public find themselves obstructed, but that one or more members of the public find themselves obstructed in the exercise of a right that belongs to the public as such. The definitions in *Archbold*, and in the 1879 draft Criminal Code, both reflect this distinction.

2.23   Another kind of public nuisance is that which affects the amenity of a neighbourhood, for example by producing noise or smells. This too has a certain analogy to private nuisance, where the activities affect the enjoyment of a neighbouring occupier. However, this analogy is not followed so far as to require injury to the enjoyment of "public property", or to make it sufficient that the noxious effect extended to a place to which the public had access. It appears to be a requirement that a sufficiently large section of the public is in fact affected. Romer LJ, in *PYA Quarries*, said:

> I do not propose to attempt a more precise definition of a public nuisance than those which emerge from the textbooks and authorities to which I have referred. It is, however, clear, in my opinion, that any nuisance is "public" which materially affects the reasonable comfort and convenience of life of a class of Her Majesty's subjects. The sphere of the nuisance may be described generally as "the neighbourhood"; but the question whether the local community within that sphere comprises a sufficient number of persons to constitute a class of the public is a question of fact in every case. It is not necessary, in my judgment, to prove that every member of the class has been injuriously affected; it is sufficient to show that a representative cross-section of the class has been so affected for an injunction to issue.[55]

2.24   On the facts of *PYA Quarries*, the vibration and dust affected the residents of about 30 houses and parts of the public highway; this may be taken to be a sufficiently large sample for the purpose. By contrast, in *Lloyd*[56] a noise affecting only three houses was held to be only a private nuisance, if that.

2.25   A third kind of public nuisance consists of offensive behaviour in public.[57] It is here that the issue in *Rimmington* arises in its most significant form. The facts are summarised by Lord Bingham as follows.

> The particulars were that he [Rimmington]:

---

[53]   Para 32.2.2 (p 1092).

[54]   Romer LJ makes the same point in *PYA Quarries* [1957] 2 QB 169, 182.

[55]   P 184.

[56]   (1802) Esp 200; cited in *PYA Quarries*, p 182 and *Smith and Hogan*, para 32.2.2 (p 1092).

[57]   At para 2.46 below, we distinguish between environmental and behavioural nuisances, and suggest that different considerations apply to the two categories.

"between 25 May 1992 and 13 June 2001, caused a nuisance to the public, namely by sending 538 separate postal packages, as detailed in the schedule ... containing racially offensive material to members of the public selected by reason of their perceived ethnicity or for their support for such a group or randomly selected in an attempt to gain support for his views, the effect of which was to cause annoyance, harassment, alarm and/or distress."

No evidence has yet been called or facts formally admitted, but it is not effectively in dispute that Mr Rimmington sent the packages listed in the schedule to the identified recipients, some of them prominent public figures, between the dates specified. The communications were strongly racist in content, crude, coarse, insulting and in some instances threatening and arguably obscene.

2.26   The prosecution relied on a series of cases concerning telephone calls. In *Norbury*[58] and *Johnson (Anthony)*[59] the defendants had made obscene telephone calls numbering in the hundreds to several women; in *Millward*[60] (an appeal against sentence) there were large numbers of calls, not stated to be obscene, to a single policewoman, with the probable result of disrupting the operation of the station switchboard. *Rimmington*[61] lists further instances of guilty pleas based on obscene calls, calls by animal liberationists to block a switchboard and hoax calls to the emergency services.

2.27   There can be no doubt that, in most of these cases, the requirement of annoyance or inconvenience to a sufficiently large number of people was satisfied. The dissatisfaction felt in *Rimmington* was based on the fact that the annoyance was inflicted on them singly and in series, thus not satisfying the requirement of *common* injury. If each individual call does not amount to a public nuisance, it is arbitrary to determine that, say, the hundredth call has the effect of retrospectively turning the whole series up to then into a connected course of conduct inflicting a common injury.[62] In other words, the analogy with the core form of the offence, namely the environmental and neighbourhood cases with a clear affinity to private nuisance, has been stretched too far for the telephone cases still to qualify as the same offence. The relevant paragraph[63] is worth quoting in full.

> I cannot, however, accept that *R v Norbury*[64] and *R v Johnson (Anthony)*[65] were correctly decided or that the convictions discussed in paras 23 to 27 above were soundly based (which is not, of course,

[58] [1978] Crim LR 435.

[59] [1997] 1 WLR 367.

[60] (1986) 8 Cr App R (S) 209.

[61] Para 27.

[62] *Rimmington*, para 48 (Lord Rodger).

[63] *Rimmington*, para 37 (Lord Bingham).

[64] [1978] Crim LR 435.

[65] [1997] 1 WLR 367.

to say that the defendants' conduct was other than highly reprehensible or that there were not other charges to which the defendants would have had no answer). To permit a conviction of causing a public nuisance to rest on an injury caused to separate individuals rather than on an injury suffered by the community or a significant section of it as a whole was to contradict the rationale of the offence and pervert its nature, in Convention terms to change the essential constituent elements of the offence to the detriment of the accused. The offence was cut adrift from its intellectual moorings. It is in my judgment very significant that when, in 1985, the Law Commission addressed the problem of poison-pen letters, and recommended the creation of a new offence, it did not conceive that the existing offence of public nuisance might be applicable. It is hard to resist the conclusion that the courts have, in effect, re-invented public mischief under another name. It is also hard to resist the conclusion expressed by Spencer in his article cited above:[66]

> "almost all the prosecutions for public nuisance in recent years seem to have taken place in one of two situations: first, where the defendant's behaviour amounted to a statutory offence, typically punishable with a small penalty, and the prosecutor wanted a bigger or extra stick to beat him with, and secondly, where the defendant's behaviour was not obviously criminal at all and the prosecutor could think of nothing else to charge him with."

> As interpreted and applied in the cases referred to in paras 23 to 27 above, the offence of public nuisance lacked the clarity and precision which both the law and the Convention require, as correctly suggested by the commentators in [1978] Crim LR 435, 436 and [1980] Crim LR 234, Spencer,[67] and Professor Ashworth in his commentary on the present cases at [2004] Crim LR 303, 304–306. See also McMahon & Binchy, *Law of Torts*, 3rd ed (2000), p 676, fn 6.

2.28 Accordingly the cases of *Norbury* and *Johnson* were overruled. There was no explicit disapproval of the other cases, such as *Millward*, as in these there were effects such as the blocking of switchboards which arguably did affect the public as such.

What type of injury?

2.29 The *Archbold* definition, in its 2005 form as discussed in *Rimmington*, says "to endanger the life, health, property, morals, or comfort of the public, or to obstruct the public in the exercise or enjoyment of rights common to all Her Majesty's subjects".

2.30 The mention of "morals" after "property" appears to be peculiar to *Archbold*, and presumably existed to cover old forms of public nuisance such as outraging

---

[66] [1989] CLJ 55, 77.

[67] [1989] CLJ 55, 77–79.

public decency and keeping a disorderly house. Both Lord Bingham and Lord Rodger, in the passages just cited, specifically observe that it should be omitted. The 2009 and 2010 editions of *Archbold* accordingly omit it, noting[68] that the change is required by *Rimmington* and explaining that outraging public decency and keeping a disorderly house are now offences separate from public nuisance. The other historic forms of nuisance based on the "morals" branch have generally been abolished, and in some cases replaced by statutory offences.

2.31   The other significant feature of this definition is that it is disjunctive: the reference to obstructing rights common to Her Majesty's subjects is alternative to the reference to endangering life or comfort. This contrasts with definitions such as Stephen's, which speak of causing inconvenience or damage *in* the exercise or enjoyment of those rights. *Rimmington* does not finally choose between the two formulations, but in light of the cases the *Archbold* formula seems preferable: as noted above,[69] the finding of public injury in cases such as *PYA Quarries* was based on the number of persons affected rather than on the fact that the adverse effects extended to a public place.

2.32   One other formulation, found in the draft Criminal Code of 1879[70] and since replicated in the Canadian Criminal Code,[71] envisages a two-step test. To be a public nuisance at all, an act must endanger the lives, safety, health, property or comfort of the public, or obstruct them in the exercise or enjoyment of their rights, as in the *Archbold* test. But to be criminal, it must endanger the lives, safety or health of the public or injure the person of an individual. An act that endangers property or comfort or obstructs public rights without affecting health and safety, while technically still a public nuisance, does not give rise to criminal liability.

2.33   This distinction is not reflected in *Rimmington* or in any other of the English cases. Every public nuisance is criminal, and endangering the comfort or amenity of the public, generally or in a particular area, is sufficient common injury to constitute the nuisance and therefore the offence.

How great an injury?

2.34   As we have seen, a potential loss of comfort or amenity is sufficient, without danger to life or limb. It is sometimes said that the loss of amenity, or the interference with the public's rights, must be "substantial". This however is not a quantitative measure, even an approximate one like "serious" or "more than trivial" or "of exceptional gravity". What is meant is "more than is reasonable in the circumstances". For example, the inconvenience caused to the neighbours by the repair of a house or the making of a delivery is justifiable provided that it is not prolonged beyond what is reasonably needed for the purpose.[72] The purpose must itself be one that is reasonable given the type of environment: for example the keeping of pumas in a garden is unreasonable in itself even if everything

---

[68]   *Archbold* para 31-50.

[69]   Paras 2.23 and 2.24.

[70]   See *Rimmington* para 10.

[71]   Para 2.64 below.

[72]   *Jones* (1812) 3 Camp 230, cited *Smith and Hogan* 32.2.1.4 (pp 1091-2).

done was reasonably required given that purpose.[73] The test appears to be the same as for the tort of private nuisance.[74]

How long?

2.35 We have seen above[75] that a public nuisance may consist of a single act as opposed to a course of conduct. It seems, however, that most cases of public nuisance consist either of a continuing series of acts or a continuing omission, or of a single act with an effect that lasts for a significant time.[76]

The fault element

2.36 The fault element of public nuisance is discussed in detail in *Rimmington and Goldstein*,[77] which also gives some account of the earlier cases on the subject. The fault element was the main issue in the *Goldstein* half of the appeal.

2.37 The facts of *Goldstein* were that Mr Goldstein, a supplier of kosher food in Manchester, sent a cheque to one of his suppliers, enclosing a small quantity of salt as a joking reference to the age of the debt, salt being commonly used as a preservative. It was also intended as an allusion to the then current anthrax scare, which the two men had discussed on the telephone shortly before. At the sorting office, the salt leaked: the postal worker, suspecting it to be anthrax, raised the alarm and the building was evacuated, causing the work of the office to be disrupted and the second postal delivery of the day to be cancelled.

2.38 The House of Lords affirmed[78] that the correct test was that laid down in *Shorrock*,[79] namely that

> the defendant is responsible for a nuisance which he knew, or ought to have known (because the means of knowledge were available to him), would be the consequence of what he did or omitted to do.

However, they held that this test was not satisfied on the facts of *Goldstein*, as there was no reason to suppose that he knew or should have known that the salt would leak, even if he knew or should have known that *if* the salt leaked, the probable consequences were the ones which occurred.[80]

2.39 They specifically declined[81] the invitation to disapprove *Shorrock* and substitute the recklessness test in *R v G*.[82] On the facts, this made no difference to the result. We discuss that test fully in Part 5 below: for the moment, it is sufficient to

---

[73] *Wheeler, The Times* 17 December 1971.

[74] For this, see *Clerk and Lindsell on Torts* (19th edition) para 20-35 and cases there cited.

[75] Para 2.13.

[76] See the list of instances in *Smith and Hogan*, para 32.2.1.1 (pp 1089-90).

[77] *Rimmington*, paras 39, 56.

[78] *Rimmington* para 39 (Bingham), 56 (Rodger)

[79] [1994] QB 279.

[80] *Rimmington*, para 40 (Bingham), 57 (Rodger).

[81] *Rimmington*, para 56 (Rodger).

[82] [2003] UKHL 50, [2004] 1 AC 1034.

state that recklessness, in this connection, means that the defendant was aware of the possible results of his or her actions and nevertheless unjustifiably went ahead. This differs from the *Shorrock* test by not including cases where the defendant did not know but ought to have done. The distinction is sometimes described as being between a "subjective" test (actual knowledge) and an "objective" one (ought to have known). The judgments in *Rimmington* did not address the question of which test would be preferable, but confined themselves to the points that the objective test was consistent with previous authority and that the issue in *G* was limited to the meaning of the word "reckless" where this was specifically mentioned by statute.

2.40   The facts of *Shorrock* were that the defendant allowed his field to be used over the weekend for a party, at which loud music was played. (The facts of the other case cited, *Ruffell*,[83] were similar but as this was an appeal against sentence the point was not argued.) It was held that he had the means of knowing that this would occur, and that the state of mind required for the offence of public nuisance was identical to that for the tort of private or public nuisance. The judgment concluded as follows.

> Indeed, given that the common law criminal offence is the causing of a public nuisance simpliciter, it would, in our judgment, be a surprising result to find that proof of the facts which would have entitled the Attorney-General to succeed in a relator action against the landowner concerned may not be sufficient to found an indictment for the criminal offence. We conclude that this is not the true position. Accordingly, in our judgment, the trial judge was correct in his direction that the appellant was guilty of the offence charged if either he knew or he ought to have known, in the sense that the means of knowledge were available to him, that there was a real risk that the consequences of the licence granted by him in respect of his field would be to create the sort of nuisance that in fact occurred, and that the judge was accordingly right to have rejected the appellant's submission to the contrary.

2.41   This test was derived from the earlier case of *Sedleigh–Denfield v O'Callaghan*[84] in which it was held that there was liability if the owner either knew or should be taken as knowing of the nuisance and nevertheless did not correct it.

2.42   In brief, the offence of public nuisance is established whenever the tort of public nuisance exists. A superficial reading of the history of the offence set out in *Rimmington* may give the impression of convergence between public nuisance and other criminal offences, as the test moves from apparently strict liability to negligence. The later cases do indeed clarify that public nuisance is not an offence of strict liability, but only because the tort itself contains a negligence test: the definition of the crime, as to the fault as well as the conduct element, remains identical to that of the tort.

2.43   The dependence of the offence on the tort is also shown by the existence of vicarious liability. In *Stephens*[85] it was held that the owner of a slate quarry was

---

[83]   (1991) 13 Cr App R (S) 204.

[84]   [1940] AC 880.

responsible for a nuisance caused by his workmen (obstruction of a river), even contrary to his orders. Mellor J observed:

> It is quite true that this in point of form is a proceeding of a criminal nature, but in substance I think it is in the nature of a civil proceeding, and I can see no reason why a different rule should prevail with regard to such an act as is charged in this indictment between proceedings which are civil and proceedings which are criminal. *I think there may be nuisances of such a character that the rule I am applying here, would not be applicable to them* (our italics), but here it is perfectly clear that the only reason for proceeding criminally is that the nuisance, instead of being merely a nuisance affecting an individual, or one or two individuals, affects the public at large, and no private individual, without receiving some special injury, could have maintained an action. Then if the contention of those who say the direction is wrong is to prevail, the public would have great difficulty in getting redress. The object of this indictment is to prevent the recurrence of the nuisance. The prosecutor cannot proceed by action, but must proceed by indictment, and if this were strictly a criminal proceeding the prosecution would be met with the objection that there was no mens rea: that the indictment charged the defendant with a criminal offence, when in reality there was no proof that the defendant knew of the act, or that he himself gave orders to his servants to do the particular act he is charged with …

2.44 The implication is that, in this case, a prosecution for public nuisance was criminal in form but tortious in substance: criminal proceedings were only brought because there was no such thing as an action for tort brought by the public. It should be noted that this does not necessarily apply to all public nuisances: for example, a nuisance consisting of offensive behaviour in public, being a wilful rather than a negligent act, would probably have been treated as genuinely criminal, so that vicarious liability would not apply.[86] The same possible distinction was adverted to in *Sherras v De Rutzen*,[87] in which it was held that a mens rea requirement applied to most offences, with some exceptions including "some, and perhaps all, public nuisances".

2.45 Recent cases including *Rimmington* do not provide certainty on whether the distinction exists, or indeed on whether vicarious criminal liability for public nuisance survives. On the one hand *Smith and Hogan* observes that "*Shorrock* suggests that the courts will not distinguish between different types of nuisance and that all will be held to impose vicarious liability".[88] On the other Lord Bingham observed that the vicarious liability cases such as *Stephens* "are hard to reconcile with the modern approach to that subject in cases potentially involving

---

[85] (1865-66) LR 1 QB 702.

[86] The distinction may be that set out in para 2.11 above between "core" nuisances to a neighbourhood and public order offences classified with nuisance for convenience.

[87] [1895] 1 QB 918.

[88] Para 32.2.4 (p 1094).

the severest penalties, and may well be explained, as Mellor J did ..., by the civil colour of the proceedings".[89]

CURRENT PRACTICE

2.46 Today public nuisance may still conveniently be divided into two categories, though the classification is different from the historical one given above.[90] The first is "environmental" nuisance, such as harmful substances and smells and obstructing the highway. The second is "behavioural" nuisance, covering offensive behaviour in public. This class is narrowed but not abolished by *Rimmington*: the test is that the offending behaviour affects several people at once and is not a mere series of acts that annoy individuals. There is some overlap between the two categories: for example drug dealing and the holding of noisy parties in public both affect the amenities of an area and are offensive in themselves.

2.47 Environmental nuisances are largely dealt with by local authorities, though usually through statutory powers and offences[91] rather than as public nuisance at common law. Most of these powers involve the use of either licensing schemes or enforcement notices. On consulting a sample of local authorities, we are informed that the normal strategy is to discuss the problem with the person responsible for a nuisance before issuing an enforcement notice: only a small proportion of cases result in prosecution for breach of the notice, and a still smaller proportion in prosecution for common law nuisance.

2.48 This is in keeping with the approach of local authorities in landlord cases and consumer product safety cases, variously known as the "compliance" strategy, as "responsive regulation" and as "smart regulation".[92] Under these strategies, local authorities apply a pyramid of measures ranging from purely voluntary and informal approaches through regulatory notices to prosecution as a last resort.[93] These are applied with discretion, as part of a compliance strategy, and having regard to the degree of risk and the level of fault. A local authority's responsibilities for public nuisance extend beyond the field of environmental regulation: for example, under the Licensing Act 2003 a licensing authority must carry out its functions with a view to the prevention of public nuisance.[94]

2.49 Apart from prosecutions, the other means of enforcement is by proceedings for an injunction, brought either by a person particularly affected or by the Attorney General. Proceedings by the Attorney General generally take (or took) the form of relator actions, in which the Attorney General lends his or her name to proceedings on behalf of a local authority or a person affected. The relator procedure remains in existence, but is seldom if ever used: we are informed by

[89] *Rimmington*, para 39.

[90] Para 2.11.

[91] These are set out in more detail in para 2.53 and following.

[92] For the differences between these, see Part 5 of our CP on "Encouraging Responsible Letting", Law Com CP No 181.

[93] Cartwright, "Enforcement, risk and discretion: the case of dangerous consumer products", (2006) 26 Legal Studies 524; Cowan and Marsh, "There's Regulatory Crime, and then there's Landlord Crime: from 'Rachmanites' to 'Partners'", (2001) 64 MLR 831.

[94] Licensing Act 2003 s 4(2)(c).

the Attorney General's office that they receive a few requests each year but have not given consent for a number of years.

2.50 Section 222 of the Local Government Act 1972 gives local authorities the power to bring civil or criminal proceedings in their own name, though it does not specifically mention either public nuisance or relator actions. Local authorities now use this power to seek injunctions against public nuisances in their own name.[95] Our consultation with local authorities indicates that this is uncommon. Instances when this power might be used are where a person has repeatedly been prosecuted for noise nuisance but continues perpetrating it, and to restrain drug dealing.[96] In short, the common law offence of public nuisance, as distinct from the various statutory nuisances, is used by local authorities for cases where the environmental and the behavioural types of nuisance overlap.

2.51 Behavioural nuisance proper is dealt with by the police and the Crown Prosecution Service by means of the common law offence. These prosecutions are comparatively frequent,[97] though in many cases public nuisance is charged in addition to statutory offences. Examples of public nuisance prosecuted by the CPS include the following:

(1) climbing on cranes or motorway bridges as a political protest;

(2) exposure in public, harassment of females;

(3) disorderly behaviour involving drugs;

(4) bomb hoaxes, false calls to the police.

Some of these instances may now fall outside the offence following *Rimmington*.

ALTERNATIVES TO PUBLIC NUISANCE

2.52 One of the criticisms made of the law of public nuisance is that all or most instances are adequately covered by other offences or statutory mechanisms. In this section we set out those offences and statutory mechanisms that are most likely to overlap with public nuisance. This should enable us not only to assess whether that criticism is justified, but also to decide whether particular features of public nuisance (for example the fault element) should be assimilated with the corresponding features of similar offences, or else made more different so as to avoid overlap.

Environmental nuisance

2.53 The most closely comparable statutory scheme is probably the Environmental Protection Act 1990, covering the following matters.

(1) Controls on pollution, by way of a regime of prescribed processes, prescribed substances, authorisations, enforcement notices, prohibition

---

[95] *Solihull Council v Maxfern Ltd* [1977] 2 All ER 177, [1977] 1 WLR 127.

[96] *Nottingham City Council v Zain* [2001] EWCA Civ 1248, [2002] 1 WLR 607.

[97] The CPS has informed us that it brought 663 prosecutions for public nuisance between April 2007 and October 2009.

notices, and offences consisting of the contravention of any of these notices.

(2) A licensing system for waste disposal and landfill.

(3) A system for identifying and remedying contaminated land, again through notices and penalties for contravention.

(4) Most relevant for our purposes, a definition of "statutory nuisance",[98] other than those arising from contaminated land.

(5) Finally, there are provisions for litter, radioactive substances and a few other miscellaneous matters.

2.54 Statutory nuisances are defined as:

79. Statutory nuisances and inspections therefor

(1) [Subject to subsections [(1ZA)][99] to (6A) below],[100] the following matters constitute "statutory nuisances" for the purposes of this Part, that is to say—

(a) any premises in such a state as to be prejudicial to health or a nuisance;

(b) smoke emitted from premises so as to be prejudicial to health or a nuisance;

(c) fumes or gases emitted from premises so as to be prejudicial to health or a nuisance;

(d) any dust, steam, smell or other effluvia arising on industrial, trade or business premises and being prejudicial to health or a nuisance;

(e) any accumulation or deposit which is prejudicial to health or a nuisance;

... [101]

(f) any animal kept in such a place or manner as to be prejudicial to health or a nuisance;

[(fa) any insects emanating from relevant industrial, trade or business premises and being prejudicial to health or a nuisance;

... [102]

---

[98] Section 79.

[99] Scotland only.

[100] Words substituted by Environment Act 1995 s 120 and Sch 22 para 89(2).

[101] Words omitted extend to Scotland only.

21

(fb)   artificial light emitted from premises so as to be prejudicial to health or a nuisance;][103]

... [104]

(g) noise emitted from premises so as to be prejudicial to health or a nuisance;

[(ga)   noise that is prejudicial to health or a nuisance and is emitted from or caused by a vehicle, machinery or equipment in a street ...[105];][106]

(h) any other matter declared by any enactment to be a statutory nuisance.

2.55   The normal procedure for dealing with a statutory nuisance is for the local authority to serve an abatement notice: it is required to do this as soon as possible after notification of the nuisance, though it sometimes delays for up to seven days to allow the offending proprietor to deal with the problem. A private individual may also apply to a magistrates' court for an abatement order. Failure to comply with an abatement order is an offence, though there is no offence of "statutory nuisance" as such. Given these powers, local authorities seldom if ever deal with statutory nuisances by way of injunctions.

2.56   The other main mechanism is the making of local authority byelaws,[107] where again the statutory power specifically refers to the suppression of nuisances; there are also powers to make byelaws under other statutes. "Nuisances" in this context appear to cover offensive or inconvenient behaviour as well as environmental nuisances. At present breach of a byelaw is a summary offence which must be prosecuted in court, though the penalty is in some instances a fixed one. The Department of Communities and Local Government is currently consulting on a new procedure, to be introduced by regulations, allowing local authorities to make byelaws on certain subjects without confirmation by the Secretary of State, and allowing those byelaws to be enforced by on-the-spot fines.[108]

2.57   Local authorities have the power to apply for injunctions against any offence that might affect local residents, as well as against non-criminal wrongs which might amount to a nuisance.[109] Examples include Sunday trading, breaches of planning law, breaches of tree preservation orders, breaches of noise abatement notices, unlicensed street trading, unlicensed sex shops, breach of trading

---

[102] Words omitted extend to Scotland only.

[103] Inserted by Clean Neighbourhoods and Environment Act 2005 s 101(1) and (2).

[104] Words omitted extend to Scotland only.

[105] Words omitted extend to Scotland only.

[106] Inserted by Noise and Statutory Nuisance Act 1993 s 2(1) and (2)(b).

[107] Local Government Act 1972 s 235 and following.

[108] http://www.communities.gov.uk/publications/localgovernment/byelaws.

[109] Local Government Act 1972 s 222.

standards, breaches of licensing laws and anti-social behaviour whether or not amounting to an offence. In the case of statutory offences, it is held that the better practice is not to apply for an injunction until all other enforcement mechanisms, including enforcement notices and prosecutions, have been tried and have proved ineffective.[110] However, this is not a legal requirement, and in some instances, such as unlawful trading or building, an injunction is granted straight away if the available penalty is clearly less than the profit that would be made by the offence, or if the act to be restrained would have irreparable consequences.[111] Nor does this inhibition appear to apply to public nuisance: according to Spencer,[112] the injunction procedure has historically been generally used in preference to prosecution.

2.58   Further offences relevant to environmental nuisance are mentioned in *Rimmington*.[113] They include polluting controlled waters[114] and obstructing the highway.[115]

Behavioural nuisance

2.59   Relevant statutory offences at the behavioural end of the spectrum are as follows.

   (1)   Violent disorder under section 2 of the Public Order Act 1986 (can only be committed by 3 or more).

   (2)   Affray under section 3 of that Act.

   (3)   Threatening or abusive behaviour under section 4, 4A or 5 of that Act.[116]

   (4)   Drunk and disorderly behaviour under section 91 of the Criminal Justice Act 1967.

   (5)   Harassment under section 1 of the Protection from Harassment Act 1997.

   (6)   Indecent exposure under section 66 of the Sexual Offences Act 2003, or voyeurism under section 67 of that Act.

   (7)   Holding raves in breach of statutory requirements under section 63 of the Criminal Justice and Public Order Act 1994.

   (8)   Bomb hoaxes under section 51 of the Criminal Law Act 1977.

---

[110] *Stoke-on-Trent City Council v B & Q (Retail) Ltd* [1984] Ch 1.

[111] *Encyclopedia of Local Government Law* vol 1, notes on Local Government Act 1972 s 222.

[112] [1989] CLJ 55, 70.

[113] Para 29.

[114] Water Resources Act 1991 s 85.

[115] Highways Act 1980 s 137.

[116] The offence under s 4 of the Act relates to conduct causing "fear or provocation of violence" whereas the offences under ss 4A and 5 relate to conduct causing "harassment, alarm and distress".

(9)   Sending items purporting to be noxious substances under section 114 of the Anti-terrorism, Crime and Security Act 2001.

(10)   Sending dangerous or noxious things through the post under section 85 of the Postal Services Act 2000.

(11)   Poison pen letters under section 1 of the Malicious Communications Act 1988.

Following *Rimmington*, some of these (in particular the last) may no longer overlap with public nuisance.

2.60   Also at the behavioural end of the spectrum is the conduct addressed by the ASBO (anti-social behaviour order) procedure. Section 1 of the Crime and Disorder Act 1998 provides as follows.

1. Anti-social behaviour orders

(1) An application for an order under this section may be made by a relevant authority if it appears to the authority that the following conditions are fulfilled with respect to any person aged 10 or over, namely—

   (a) that the person has acted, since the commencement date, in an anti-social manner, that is to say, in a manner that caused or was likely to cause harassment, alarm or distress to one or more persons not of the same household as himself; and

   (b) that such an order is necessary to protect relevant persons from further anti-social acts by him.

...

(3) Such an application shall be made by complaint to a magistrates' court.

(4) If, on such an application, it is proved that the conditions mentioned in subsection (1) above are fulfilled, the magistrates' court may make an order under this section (an "anti-social behaviour order") which prohibits the defendant from doing anything described in the order.

...

(6) The prohibitions that may be imposed by an anti-social behaviour order are those necessary for the purpose of protecting persons (whether relevant persons or persons elsewhere in England and Wales) from further anti-social acts by the defendant.

(7) An anti-social behaviour order shall have effect for a period (not less than two years) specified in the order or until further order.

...

(10) If without reasonable excuse a person does anything which he is prohibited from doing by an anti-social behaviour order, he [is guilty of an offence and][117] liable—

    (a) on summary conviction, to imprisonment for a term not exceeding six months or to a fine not exceeding the statutory maximum, or to both; or

    (b) on conviction on indictment, to imprisonment for a term not exceeding five years or to a fine, or to both.

It has been held that, where the ASBO procedure is available, it is inappropriate to seek an injunction instead.[118] This point would apply equally to injunctions to restrain criminal behaviour and injunctions to restrain a public nuisance.

OTHER COUNTRIES

2.61 In the Australian states, nuisance is defined at common law in the same way as in England and Wales, though some states have codified their criminal law.[119] In addition, some states (e.g. Queensland) have a statutory "public nuisance offence", covering offensive language and behaviour in public.[120] As stated above,[121] in England and Wales many of these instances would be covered by specific statutory offences; but the current, as opposed to the older,[122] legislative practice in England and Wales is to make these offences entirely separate rather than creating statutory forms of public nuisance.

2.62 New Zealand defines "criminal nuisance" in s 145 of the Crimes Act 1961.

Criminal nuisance

141.—(1) Every one commits criminal nuisance who does any unlawful act or omits to discharge any legal duty, such act or omission being one which he knew would endanger the lives, safety, or health of the public, or the life, safety, or health of any individual.

(2) Every one who commits criminal nuisance is liable to imprisonment for a term not exceeding 1 year.

2.63 This is narrower than the English offence, in that it requires danger to life, safety or health as a condition of criminal liability. Mere loss of amenity is not enough. The mental element is stringent: the statute specifies that the defendant "knew"

---

[117] Words substituted by Police Reform Act 2002 s 61(1) and (8).

[118] *Birmingham City Council v Shaffi and Ellis* [2008] EWCA Civ 1186, [2009] 3 All ER 127.

[119] David Barker, *Essential Australian Law* (2000) p 123. "A public nuisance is a crime, punishable at common law on indictment. It is also provided for in the Criminal Codes of Queensland, Western Australia, Tasmania and the Northern Territory."

[120] Summary Offences Act 2005 s 6 (discussed Walsh, "Offensive Language, Offensive Behaviour and Public Nuisance: Empirical and Theoretical Analyses", [2005] UQLJ 5). This must be distinguished from public nuisance as such, as defined in s 230 of the Queensland Criminal Code: *Rimmington* para 11.

[121] Para 2.59.

[122] For which see Spencer, as cited in para 2.10 above.

(not believed, or was reckless, or ought to have known) that the act "would" (not could, or might, or was likely to) endanger the lives etc of others. Arguably, however, the element of potentiality is caught by the word "endanger", which includes a merely potential harm.

2.64   The Canadian criminal code defines common nuisance as follows.

> **180.**—(1) Every one who commits a common nuisance and thereby
>
>   (a) endangers the lives, safety or health of the public, or
>
>   (b) causes physical injury to any person,
>
> is guilty of an indictable offence and liable to imprisonment for a term not exceeding two years.
>
>   (2) For the purposes of this section, every one commits a common nuisance who does an unlawful act or fails to discharge a legal duty and thereby
>
>   (a) endangers the lives, safety, health, property or comfort of the public; or
>
>   (b) obstructs the public in the exercise or enjoyment of any right that is common to all the subjects of Her Majesty in Canada.

2.65   The basic definition of nuisance is similar to the English, in that it includes acts endangering the property or comfort of the public or obstructing public rights such as highways. However, it is not made criminal unless it endangers life, safety or health or causes an injury. This follows the two-step test in the draft Criminal Code of 1879:[123] in effect, the conditions for criminal liability are as narrow as in the New Zealand offence.

2.66   It should be noted that Stephen's definition, "act not warranted by law" has been replaced by the narrower phrase "unlawful act". In the case of *Thornton*,[124] concerning a person who had donated blood while infected by HIV, the two limbs of the definition were considered separately. "Unlawful act" was interpreted literally, as meaning conduct specifically proscribed by legislation. A "legal duty", on the other hand, was held to extend to a common law duty of care, and was therefore sufficient to cover the facts of the case.

2.67   The Canadian definition is silent on the fault element of the offence. In *Thornton*, the defendant appealed on the ground that the judge had mistakenly applied an objective instead of a subjective test in deciding on the fault element of the offence.[125] The Ontario Court of Appeal did not decide which test was correct, but assumed a subjective test for the purposes of argument: it was held that the judge had not in fact applied an objective test and that a subjective test would be

---

[123] Para 2.32 above.

[124] (1991) 3 CR (4th) 381; affirmed by the Supreme Court of Canada [1993] 2 SCR 445.

[125] For these tests, see para 2.39 above.

satisfied on the facts of the case. The offence is very rarely used, as most instances of nuisance are dealt with by civil proceedings at provincial level.

2.68   In the United States the tort of public nuisance is defined in much the same way as in England and Wales. As a crime, it forms part of the description of several statutory offences under the codes of particular states; older examples concern keeping a disorderly house and other offences against public morals, while newer examples are often concerned with inner city gang activity. The injunction procedure has been held lawful in this connection.[126]

[126] *People ex rel Gallo v Acuna* (1997) 14 Cal 4th 1090, 60 Cal Rptr 2d 277; 929 P 2d 596.

PART 3
OUTRAGING PUBLIC DECENCY: THE EXISTING LAW

3.1   The offence of outraging public decency appears to consist of performing any indecent activity in such a place or way that more than one member of the public may witness and be disgusted by it.   As it was put in *Hamilton*, the leading modern case on the offence:[1]

> These cases established that, if the offence of outraging public decency were to be proved, it was necessary to prove two elements. (i) The act was of such a lewd character as to outrage public decency; this element constituted the nature of the act which had to be proved before the offence could be established; (ii) it took place in a public place and must have been capable of being seen by two or more persons who were actually present, even if they had not actually seen it.

Conduct element: the activities covered

3.2   The traditional forms of the offence involve either exposing oneself (either simply, or in the act of performing a sexual activity) or creating an indecent display, for example of pictures.   Examples are as follows.

   (1)   Indecent exposure.[2]

   (2)   Performing sexual activities in public.[3]

   (3)   Nude bathing in inhabited areas.[4]

   (4)   Disinterring a corpse for dissection.[5]

   (5)   Exhibition of sculpture consisting of human head with freeze-dried human foetuses as earrings.[6]

   (6)   Urinating on a war memorial while drunk.[7]

---

[1]   [2007] EWCA Crim 2062, [2008] QB 224 para 21 (CA).

[2]   *Sidley* (1663) 1 Sid 168; *Watson* (1847) 2 Cox CC 376; *Holmes* (1853) 1 Dears CC 207; *Thallman* (1863) 9 Cox CC 388; *Wellard* (1884–85) LR 14 QBD 63; *Walker* [1996] 1 Cr App Rep 111, CA.

[3]   *Bunyan* (1844) 1 Cox CC 74; *Orchard* (1848) 3 Cox CC 248; *Elliot* (1861) Le & Ca 103; *Harris* (1871) LR 1 CCR 282; *Mayling* [1963] 2 QB 717, 47 Cr App Rep 102, CCA; *May* (1989) 91 Cr App Rep 157, [1990] Crim LR 415, CA; *Rose v DPP* [2006] EWHC 852 (Admin), [2006] 1 WLR 2626, [2006] 2 Cr App R 29, QBD.

[4]   *Crunden* (1809) 2 Camp 89; *Reed* (1871) 12 Cox CC 1.

[5]   *Lynn* (1788) 2 Term Rep 733.

[6]   *Gibson, Sylveire* [1990] 2 QB 619, [1991] 1 All ER 439, 91 Cr App R 341 CA

[7]   *Laing* (unreported guilty plea) http://www.timesonline.co.uk/tol/news/uk/crime/article6933293.ece.

3.3 A controversial area is that of publications, which was discussed in full in *Knuller (Publishing, Printing and Promotions) Ltd v DPP*.[8] The facts concerned a magazine containing a number of contact advertisements for homosexuals. The defendant was charged with conspiracy to corrupt public morals and conspiracy to outrage public decency.[9] Lord Diplock, dissenting, devoted most of his discussion to the first count, holding that *Shaw v DPP*,[10] which affirmed the existence of that offence, should be overruled; but he also held that the issues in the two offences were logically indistinguishable.

> The old judicial dicta which in *Shaw's case* were treated as the historical justification for holding that an agreement to do anything which tended to corrupt public morals amounts to a crime at common law, do not, as I hope to show, draw any distinction between conduct or conspiracies directed against public morals and conduct or conspiracies directed against public decency. As a matter of decision *Shaw's case* was limited to conspiracies to corrupt public morals: as a matter of judicial reasoning its scope cannot logically be so confined. To bow to the decision yet to deny the legal reasoning upon which it was based is to draw the kind of distinction which reflects discredit on the English legal system.[11]

It followed that in his view neither of the offences was known to the law.

3.4 Lord Reid regretfully held that the existence of conspiracy to corrupt public morals was established by *Shaw* and that the House of Lords ought not to overrule it. Outraging public decency was in his view confined to the two categories of indecent exposure and indecent displays: there was no generalised offence of outraging public decency, still less of conspiracy to do so.

> The second count is conspiracy to outrage public decency, the particulars, based on the same facts, being that the accused conspired with persons inserting lewd disgusting and offensive advertisements in the magazine "by means of the publication of the said magazine containing the said advertisements to outrage public decency."

> The crucial question here is whether in this generalised form this is an offence known to the law. There are a number of particular offences well known to the law which involve indecency in various ways but none of them covers the facts of this case. We were informed that a charge of this character has never been brought with regard to printed matter on sale to the public.

---

[8] [1973] AC 435, [1972] 3 All ER 898.

[9] The distinction is that "corrupting public morals" refers to matter liable to corrupt and deprave, while "outraging public decency" refers to matter liable to shock and disgust: see para 3.20 below. Corrupting public morals, as distinct from conspiracy to do so, is not in itself an offence at common law.

[10] [1962] AC 220. This case concerned the publication of the "Ladies' Directory", which was a list of contact details of prostitutes.

[11] [1973] AC 435, 469.

...

I think that the objections to the creation of this generalised offence are similar in character to but even greater than the objections to the generalised offence of conspiracy to corrupt public morals.

...

There are at present three well-known offences of general application which involve indecency: indecent exposure of the person, keeping a disorderly house, and exposure or exhibition in public of indecent things or acts. The first two are far removed from sale of indecent literature and I can see no real analogy with the third.

Indecent exhibitions in public have been widely interpreted. Indecency is not confined to sexual indecency: indeed it is difficult to find any limit short of saying that it includes anything which an ordinary decent man or woman would find to be shocking, disgusting and revolting. And "in public" also has a wide meaning. It appears to cover exhibitions in all places to which the public have access either as of right or gratis or on payment. There is authority to the effect that two or more members of the public must be able to see the exhibition at the same time, but I doubt whether that applies in all cases. We were not referred to any case where the exhibition consisted of written or printed matter but it may well be that public exhibition of an indecent notice or advertisement would be punishable.

But to say that an inside page of a book or magazine exposed for sale is exhibited in public seems to me to be going far beyond both the general purpose and intendment of this offence and any decision or even dictum in any case.[12]

3.5 According to the majority in that case, however, it can also extend to other visible manifestations, including publishing a book or a magazine. Lord Morris of Borth-y-Gest held that the offence was not confined to "displays" in the sense of things immediately visible in public:

It seems to me to be wholly unrealistic to say that if a magazine which is sold in public has matter on its outside cover which outrages public decency (which means outrages the sense of decency of members of the public) an offence is then committed, whereas if the outside cover of the magazine is plain and innocuous but if as soon as the magazines are opened the members of the public who buy them are outraged by all that they see, then no offence is committed.[13]

Lord Simon of Glaisdale, similarly, considered that the various authorities cited established the existence of a broad offence of outraging public decency, rather than a series of piecemeal offences such as indecent exposure and indecent

[12] [1973] AC 435, 457-8.

[13] [1973] AC 435, 467-8.

displays, and that the fact that the offence had not hitherto been applied to the contents of books and newspapers did not mean that it could not be so applied:

> It is, in general, the difference between mature and rudimentary legal systems that the latter deal specifically with a number of particular and unrelated instances, whereas the former embody the law in comprehensive, cohesive and rational general rules. The law is then easier to understand and commands a greater respect. Fragmentation, on the other hand, leads to anomalous (and therefore inequitable) distinctions and to hedging legal rules round with technicalities that are only within the understanding of an esoteric class. The general development of English law (like that of other mature systems) has been towards the co-ordination of particular instances into comprehensive and comprehensible general rules.[14]

Interestingly, he holds that, if it were not possible to group all the disparate instances into an offence of outraging public decency, they would be forms of public nuisance.[15]

However, the appeal on the second count was allowed because there had been a misdirection on the meaning of "decency".

3.6   The cases mostly relate to activities with visible manifestations, which may disgust members of the public who see them. In *Hamilton*,[16] the court observed:

> There is no reason why in principle the nature of the act cannot be witnessed in another way such as hearing; we therefore accept the argument of the prosecution that the nature of the act can be capable of being witnessed by means other than seeing.

The main issue in the case, namely whether it is necessary that the act was actually witnessed as opposed to being capable of being witnessed, is discussed below.[17]

3.7   Further instances of the offence involve taking intimate photographs of women without their consent. In *Choi*[18] the defendant went into a cubicle in a ladies' lavatory in a supermarket and filmed a lady in the next cubicle; she saw the lens or the mirror attached to the lens and called for help. In *Hamilton* the defendant attached a hidden video camera to a rucksack and used it to film up the skirts of women and girls in supermarkets. Neither of these cases involved the intentional creation of an indecent display, but both involved acts which could cause outrage if detected.

---

[14]   [1973] AC 435, 492.

[15]   [1973] AC 435, 493.

[16]   [2007] EWCA Crim 2062, [2008] QB 224 para 34.

[17]   Para 3.30 and following.

[18]   *Choi* [1999] EWCA Crim 1279, [1999] 8 Archbold News 3, CA.

3.8   *Knuller* lists further instances which have been held to fall within the offence.[19] These are *Delaval*[20] (procuring a girl apprentice to be taken out of the custody of her master for the purpose of prostitution) and *Howell and Bentley*[21] (conspiracy to procure a girl of 17 to become a common prostitute); *Delaval* also mentions the sale of a wife as an example. The common element in these cases is that, rather than being likely to produce reactions of shock or disgust in the witnesses, the defendant's actions are only shocking in the abstract sense of being considered to be immoral: a person hearing about the facts may say "How shocking!" but is unlikely to feel actual shock as a result of those actions.

3.9   This distinction opens up a divergence of approach between Lord Morris and Lord Simon. For Lord Morris, the facts in *Knuller* fall within the offence because it is artificial to distinguish between the inside of a magazine and the outside: the offence is simply a logical extension of Lord Reid's category of indecent display. For Lord Simon, the corruption of public morals and the outraging of public decency extend to all forms of public immorality and, together with public nuisance, are particular forms of the overarching category of public mischief.[22] As Lord Reid and Lord Diplock dissented, and Lord Kilbrandon agreed with Lord Simon, this must be taken as the ground of the decision.

3.10   The distinction between the positions of Lord Morris and Lord Simon is very like that raised in public nuisance. As we saw,[23] in *Rimmington* the House of Lords decided that public nuisance only extended to cases within an easy extension of the environmental cases with a clear analogy to private nuisance, and that to make it more general than this was to cut the offence adrift from its intellectual moorings and to reinvent public mischief. In the same way, one could paraphrase Lord Morris as saying that outraging public decency should be confined to cases with a clear analogy to indecent display, and that to extend it wider (for example to include the procuring cases) is to cut it adrift from its intellectual moorings. Equally, in *Knuller* the argument was raised that public mischief and its subdivisions were not so much an offence as a residual power of creating new offences, and it was held that, however that may have been once, the categories are now fixed.[24]

3.11   Since *Knuller* was decided, the House of Lords has decided, in *Withers*,[25] that public mischief is not an offence known to the law. Together with *Rimmington*, this may indicate that Lord Morris' reasoning should now be preferred as the basis for the offence of outraging public decency. This accords with the ruling in *Hamilton* that, in addition to being indecent as a matter of description, the acts in

---

[19]   [1973] AC 435, 493.

[20]   (1763) 3 Burr 1434.

[21]   (1864) 4 F & F 160.

[22]   [1973] AC 435, 490-491.

[23]   Para 2.27 above.

[24]   [1973] AC 435, 490.

[25]   [1975] AC 842.

question should also have the possible consequence of causing actual shock or outrage.[26]

Conspiracy

3.12 Another complication is the relationship between outraging public decency and conspiracy to outrage public decency. The second count in *Knuller* was for conspiracy to outrage public decency. This was treated as an offence of the same sort as the first count, of conspiracy to corrupt public morals: it was not suggested that there was an offence of "corrupting public morals" on its own. On the other hand, the earlier cases, from *Sidley*[27] to *Mayling*,[28] relied on in *Knuller* to establish the existence of the offence of conspiracy to outrage public decency all concerned charges of substantive offences by individuals and not of conspiracy, and Lord Diplock[29] deplored "the device of charging a defendant with agreeing to do what he did instead of charging him with doing it".

3.13 The law of conspiracy was transformed by the Criminal Law Act 1977, which creates a statutory offence of conspiracy to commit an offence, and provides:

5. Abolitions, savings, transitional provisions, consequential amendment and repeals

(1) Subject to the following provisions of this section, the offence of conspiracy at common law is hereby abolished.

(2) Subsection (1) above shall not affect the offence of conspiracy at common law so far as relates to conspiracy to defraud ...[30]

(3) Subsection (1) above shall not affect the offence of conspiracy at common law if and in so far as it may be committed by entering into an agreement to engage in conduct which—

(a) tends to corrupt public morals or outrages public decency; but

(b) would not amount to or involve the commission of an offence if carried out by a single person otherwise than in pursuance of an agreement.

3.14 The implication is that there can be conspiracy to outrage public decency where the agreed conduct does not itself amount to the offence of outraging public decency (or any offence), since if it did amount to that offence it would be excluded by subsection (3)(b). This situation might arise if a future court held that the offence of outraging public decency did not exist or severely reduced its scope, without at the same time abolishing or reducing the scope of conspiracy to outrage public decency.

---

[26] Para 3.22 below.

[27] (1662) 1 Sid 168.

[28] [1963] 2 QB 717.

[29] [1973] AC 435, 470.

[30] Some words repealed by Criminal Justice Act 1987 s 12(2).

3.15 In *Knuller*, however, there was no suggestion that outraging public decency had a different meaning in conspiracy from that which it bore in the substantive offence. If this is correct, it would appear that there is no scope for charging common law conspiracy to outrage public decency, as it will always be possible to charge statutory conspiracy to commit the common law offence of outraging public decency.[31] Accordingly, we consider that the common law offence of conspiracy to outrage public decency serves no useful purpose and could reasonably be abolished.[32] We consider below[33] the question of whether outraging public decency should itself be restated in statutory form: if so, the two reforms could conveniently be combined.

Circumstance and consequence elements

Indecency

3.16 For an article or activity to be capable of causing public outrage two conditions must be met. It must be so indecent as to be likely to cause outrage if witnessed; and there must be the possibility that it will be witnessed. Here we discuss the first of these conditions.

3.17 In common, and often in judicial, parlance the words "indecent" and "obscene" are ambiguous. An indecent spectacle can mean either one that titillates, or one that disgusts, or one that titillates some while disgusting others, while "obscene" is simply a stronger alternative to "indecent", in both meanings. For example, Lord Parker in *Stanley*[34] said:

> The words "indecent or obscene" convey one idea, namely, offending against the recognised standards of propriety, indecent being at the lower end of the scale and obscene at the upper end of the scale.

3.18 Since the Obscene Publications Acts, however, it has sometimes been found useful to reserve "obscene" for what may corrupt and deprave, in accordance with its statutory meaning under those Acts,[35] and "indecent" for what may shock or disgust. The offence we are considering is mainly concerned with the second class: spectacles in the first class properly fall within either the Obscene Publications Acts or the offence of corrupting public morals.[36]

3.19 For this reason outraging public decency can include acts and displays that are disgusting in a non-sexual way: for example the exhuming of bodies[37] or the display of dried foetuses.[38] Other instances listed in *Knuller* are exhibiting

---

[31] *Smith and Hogan* para 13.3.4.3 (p 430-1).

[32] See our proposal at para 6.15(3) below.

[33] Para 6.12 and following.

[34] [1965] 1 All ER 1035, 1038.

[35] OPA 1959 s 1(1).

[36] In the case of a publication, *only* the Obscene Publications Acts can be used, and common law offences are excluded: OPA 1959 s 2(4). But according to *Shaw*, confirmed in *Knuller*, this only applies to publications that are "obscene" in the sense of liable to corrupt and deprave, not in the sense of liable to disgust.

[37] *Lynn* (1788) 2 Term Rep 733.

[38] *Gibson, Sylveire* [1990] 2 QB 619, [1991] 1 All ER 439, 91 Cr App R 341 (CA).

deformed children[39] and exhibiting a picture of sores.[40] As Lord Reid said in *Knuller*:[41]

> Indecency is not confined to sexual indecency: indeed it is difficult to find any limit short of saying that it includes anything which an ordinary decent man or woman would find to be shocking, disgusting and revolting.

3.20 In *Gibson and Sylveire* (the case of the foetus earrings) Lord Lane CJ said:

> There are, it seems to us, two broad types of offence involving obscenity. On the one hand are those involving the corruption of public morals, and on the other hand, and distinct from the former, are those which involve an outrage on public decency, whether or not public morals are involved.
>
> That distinction is clear, in our judgment, from the speeches of their Lordships in *Knuller*. Lord Morris of Borth-y-Gest, said, at p. 468:
>
> > It may well be that in this present case it would have been sufficient to prefer only count 1. But the conceptions of the two counts are different. Count 1 alleges an intention to debauch and corrupt. Count 2 raises the issue not whether people might be corrupted but whether the sense of decency of members of the public would be outraged.
>
> …
>
> There is no suggestion here that anyone is likely to be corrupted by the exhibiting of these earrings. It seems to us that the two types of offence are both factually and morally distinct.

3.21 The offence caused must be strong enough to amount to shock or disgust: mere distaste or embarrassment would not seem to be enough. The cases of *Choi* and *Hamilton* suggest that, in the list of relevant consequences, to shock and disgust one should add humiliation (on the part of those photographed) and indignation (on the part of bystanders).

3.22 In *Hamilton*,[42] the requirement was summed up as follows.

> The first element is one that constitutes the nature of the act which has to be proved. It has to be proved both that the act is of such a lewd, obscene or disgusting character and that it outrages public decency. (i) An obscene act is an act which offends against recognised standards of propriety and which is at a higher level of impropriety than indecency; see *R v Stanley*.[43] A disgusting act is one

---

[39] *Herring v Walround* (1681) 2 Chan Cas 110.

[40] *Grey* (1864) 4 F & F 73.

[41] Para 3.4 above.

[42] [2007] EWCA Crim 2062, [2008] QB 224 para 30.

[43] [1965] 1 All ER 1035, [1965] 2 QB 327.

"which fills the onlooker with loathing or extreme distaste or causes annoyance"; *R v Choi* (7 May 1999, unreported). It is clear that the act done by the appellant was capable of being judged by a jury to be a lewd, obscene or disgusting act. It is the nature of the act that the jury had to consider and it was clear in our view that the jury were entitled to find that it was lewd, obscene or disgusting, even if no one saw him doing it. (ii) It is not enough that the act is lewd, obscene or disgusting and that it might shock people; it must, as Lord Simon made clear in the *Knuller* case,[44] be of such a character that it outrages minimum standards of public decency as judged by the jury in contemporary society. As was pointed out, 'outrages' is a strong word.

3.23   In short, indecency is not simply a description of the nature of the object or activity: it is not sufficient that an action can be described as "shocking" in the abstract, meaning shocking to hear about. The main requirement is that the action may produce a public reaction, by actually shocking or disgusting those who witness it. That is why we consider indecency as part of the consequence element rather than the conduct element of the offence. We shall return to this point in considering the fault element of the offence, as one form of fault element is foresight of consequences.

Place

3.24   The offence must be committed "in public" in the sense of being in a public place. Lord Simon, in *Knuller*, said:

> It was argued for the Crown that it was immaterial whether or not the alleged outrage to decency took place in public, provided that the sense of decency of the public or a substantial section of the public was outraged. But this seems to me to be contrary to many of the authorities which the Crown itself relied on to establish the generic offence. The authorities establish that the word "public" has a different connotation in the respective offences of conspiracy to corrupt public morals and conduct calculated to, or conspiracy to, outrage public decency. In the first it refers to certain fundamental rules regarded as essential social control which yet lack the force of law: when applicable to individuals, in other words, "public" refers to persons in society. In the latter offences, however, "public" refers to the place in which the offence is committed.[45]

3.25   The place need not be "public" in the sense of being public property or there being a public right of way: it is sufficient if members of the public can in fact see the object or act in question, whether by going there or by looking in.[46] For this reason one can commit the offence in one's own home, if others could see in through the window;[47] or on a roof;[48] or while trespassing in fields that are private

---

[44]   [1973] AC 435, [1972] 2 All ER 898.

[45]   [1973] AC 435, 494.

[46]   *Bunyan* (1844) 1 Cox CC 74, *Wellard* (1884–85) LR 14 QBD 63.

[47]   *Rouverard* (unreported) 1830.

property but where other trespassers sometimes come;[49] or in a public lavatory[50] (though exposure as such is not covered, being expected there by reason of its function[51]). All these cases are listed and discussed in *Hamilton*,[52] which comments:

> In their very illuminating work *Rook & Ward on Sexual Offences: Law and Practice*, 3rd ed (2004), para 14.43, Peter Rook QC and Robert Ward consider that this case [*Thallman*] was an example of the court considering that the requirement that the act must be committed in a public place was falling into disfavour; they rely on dicta in other cases that they suggest support their view.

In *Wellard*[53] Huddleston B expressed the view that:

> The act was in a public and open place, and that disposes of the case, but I am by no means satisfied that indecency before several in a private place is not punishable.

This however was answered by the extract from *Knuller* set out above.

3.26 The requirement of being "in public", in the extended sense established by the cases, reinforces the point made above,[54] about indecency as a consequence element. The public must have visual or auditory access to the place where the offence was committed, so that they can be outraged in the capacity of witnesses. It is not sufficient that the act is such as to outrage the public in the sense that they would be shocked if they heard about it.

Potential witnesses

3.27 The act must be capable of being witnessed by more than one person: if only one person saw it or could have seen it, it is not sufficient. In several cases where the defendant exposed himself to one person, and there was no realistic chance that anyone else would see it, the offence was held not to have been committed.[55]

3.28 This point is illustrated in *Rose v DPP*,[56] concerning a couple who performed an act of oral sex in a bank foyer within view of a CCTV camera. The recording was seen by one bank official the following morning, some hours later, and it was accepted that the couple were completely oblivious to the camera's presence. As well as illustrating the point about only one person being in a position to witness

---

[48] *Thallman* (1863) 9 Cox CC 388.

[49] *Wellard* (1884–85) LR 14 QBD 63.

[50] *Harris* (1871) LR 1 CCR 282; *Mayling* [1963] 2 QB 717, 47 Cr App Rep 102.

[51] *Orchard* (1848) 3 Cox CC 248.

[52] Paras 20 and 21.

[53] Above; cited in *Hamilton* para 22. But compare *Walker*, para 3.29(1) below.

[54] Para 3.23.

[55] *Watson* (1847) 2 Cox CC 376; *Webb* (1848) 3 Cox CC 183, 1 Den 338, 344; *Farrell* (1862) 9 Cox CC 446.

[56] [2006] EWHC 852 (Admin), [2006] 1 WLR 2626, [2006] 2 Cr App R 29

the act, the case illustrates a further argument that the offence must be complete when committed, and cannot wait in suspense until viewing occurs some time later. *Rose* further clarifies that the potential witnesses to the act do not include a willing participant in it: the couple cannot be regarded as performing an indecent act in the view of each other (plus the person viewing the film).[57]

3.29   The "more than one person" can mean as few as two, but not simply: there must be a flavour of randomness, of "anyone could have seen it". This is connected with the requirement of a public place, meaning a place to which the public have actual or visual access.

    (1)   It does not apply to a closed audience of two persons, however unwilling, selected by the offender, where there was no possibility that anyone else would join them. For example, in *Walker*[58] a man exposed himself to his daughter and one other girl in his own living room, and this was held not to be "public" in the sense required: the two girls were members of the public, but were not there in that capacity.

    (2)   However it can apply to a case where "anyone could have come in", but only out of a restricted public such as pupils at a school.[59]

    (3)   Similarly it applies to a case where "anyone could have come in" by asking or paying for admission, as in the case of a pay-per-entry booth on Epsom Downs in which an indecent display was kept.[60] This is the justification of the publication cases such as *Knuller*, where anyone could have bought the magazine.

Whether actual witness required

3.30   We have seen that the indecent act must be performed in the potential view, and to the potential shock or disgust, of two or more people. It is not necessary that two people actually saw it and were disgusted by it, or even that two people actually saw it at all. In *Mayling*[61] it was held to be sufficient if one person saw it, whether or not that person was disgusted, but the place was open enough so that two other people *might* have come in and been disgusted.

3.31   It is necessary that the indictment should mention the possibility of disgusting the public: if it simply refers to the presence of one person, it is insufficient.[62] The conventional wording is "committed an act of a lewd obscene and disgusting nature and outraging public decency by behaving in an indecent manner at

---

[57]   Para 28 of the judgment; *Smith and Hogan* 31.3.14.1 (p 1059).

[58]   [1996] 1 Cr App Rep 111 (CA). Quaere, if the selected audience was larger: *Wellard*, above. (*Wellard* was decided on the basis that others might have passed by, but it was left open whether exposure to the invited persons might be sufficient.)

[59]   *May* (1989) 91 Cr App Rep 157, [1990] Crim LR 415 (CA).

[60]   *Saunders* (1875) 1 QBD 15, CCR.

[61]   [1963] 2 QB 717, 47 Cr App Rep 102 (CCA): for facts see para 3.32 below.

[62]   *Watson*, above.

[place] to the great disgust and annoyance of divers of Her Majesty's subjects within whose purview such behaviour was committed".[63]

3.32   In *Mayling* a person committed acts of indecency in a public lavatory in view of two police officers, who did not testify that they were disgusted; another person did come out with a look of disgust on his face, but it was accepted that that might have been attributable to the state of the lavatory. It was held that there is no necessity for any person to be actually disgusted.

> In the present case, it is to be noted that, in the particulars of offence, the act was described as "of a lewd obscene and disgusting nature and outraging public decency" and it was incumbent upon the prosecution to satisfy the jury not merely that the defendant did the act and did it in public, but also that the act was of the description alleged. The operative words, i.e., "of a lewd obscene and disgusting nature and outraging public decency," may be paraphrased without altering their effect as "such an act of a lewd obscene or disgusting nature as constitutes an outrage to public decency involving great disgust and annoyance of divers of Her Majesty's subjects." If the jury were so satisfied, the offence was proved and, in the judgment of this court, it was not necessary for the prosecution to go further and prove actual disgust or annoyance on the part of any observer.[64]

3.33   In *Lunderbech*,[65] on somewhat similar facts (but without the disgusted third party), it was held that the presence of the police officers, whether they were disgusted or not, demonstrated that it was possible for members of the public to pass by and be disgusted. Unfortunately this clearly correct proposition appears to have been confused with the distinct, and more dubious, argument that, given the nature of the act, it is a reasonable inference that the police officers were disgusted. J C Smith, in his case commentary, argues that this was a fiction intended to justify the usual form of indictment, which appears to suggest actual annoyance to the public.

3.34   The result is something of a hybrid between concrete "shock" and abstract "shockingness". The act must be in public in the sense that it is possible for members of the public to witness it. But it is not necessary to prove that *those* potential witnesses would be shocked: the standard is whether the jury think it indecent because it would shock them.[66]

3.35   As a matter of abstract law this is well established. The issue in *Mayling*, and especially in *Lunderbech*, is a little different. If the indictment, in a given case, appears to speak of the public being actually shocked or outraged, and all that is proved is that there were disgusting acts within potential public view, does it follow that the defendant should be acquitted, not because his conduct falls outside the offence but because it falls outside the indictment? Smith's answer is

---

[63]   *Mayling*, above.

[64]   *Mayling*, p 726.

[65]   [1991] Crim LR 784 (CA); otherwise unreported.

[66]   So argued in Smith's case commentary, above, and in *Smith and Hogan* para 31.3.14.1 (p 1058).

that the conventional wording, as used in *Mayling*, is a formality of pleading. However, it may be preferable to frame indictments in a broader way, by using phrases such as "of a lewd obscene and disgusting nature and outraging public decency", without stating that any of Her Majesty's subjects were actually disgusted.[67]

3.36 In short, earlier cases, culminating in *Mayling* and approved in *Knuller*, suggest that it is necessary that the act *was* witnessed by one (who need not be disgusted) and *could have been* witnessed by more (who might be disgusted). The question then arises whether the first requirement is a substantive ingredient of the offence, as establishing that the act was done in public, or only an evidential requirement, because otherwise there would be no evidence that the act was performed at all.

3.37 That was the issue in *Hamilton*.[68] As explained,[69] the defendant made a practice of filming up women's skirts in supermarkets,[70] though neither the women nor any of the bystanders were aware of his doing so and the only evidence was the defendant's recordings. The evidential requirement was therefore satisfied, and the question was whether being actually seen or heard was an essential ingredient of the offence. The court acknowledged[71] that, on the existing state of authority, the question was an open one.[72]

3.38 After a detailed review of most of the authorities, including those described above, the court considered that the purpose of the two-person rule was to establish the public nature of the act.

> In our view it is necessary to have regard to the purpose of the two-person rule; it goes solely to the necessity that there be a public element in the sense of more than one being present and capable of being affected by it. There is in our view no reason to confine the requirement more restrictively and require actual sight or sound of the nature of the act. The public element in the offence is satisfied if the act is done where persons are present and the nature of what is being done is capable of being seen; the principle is that the public are to be protected from lewd, obscene or disgusting acts which are of a nature that outrages public decency and which are capable of being seen in public. As was pointed out in *R v Bunyan*,[73] a person committing such an act may wish as much privacy as possible, if there is a possibility of them being discovered in public, it would none

---

[67] See the briefer form of words suggested in *Archbold* (20-239). But compare *Watson*, above, where an indictment only mentioning the presence of one person was held to be insufficient.

[68] [2007] EWCA Crim 2062, [2008] QB 224.

[69] Para 3.7 above.

[70] Another case of filming up skirts is *Tinsley* [2003] EWCA Crim 3032 (cited *Hamilton* para 27): as this was a guilty plea the justification for charging the offence was not discussed.

[71] *Hamilton*, paras 20(vi), 37. There was a single judgment of the court, delivered by Thomas LJ.

[72] *Elliot* (1861) Le & Ca 103 raises, but does not decide, the question whether the offence could be proved by confession evidence alone.

the less be an offence. Looking therefore at the purpose of the two-person rule, it can, in our view, be satisfied if there are two or more persons present who are capable of seeing the nature of the act, even if they did not actually see it. Moreover, the purpose of the requirement that the act be of such a kind that it outrages public decency goes, as we have said, to setting a standard which the jury must judge by reference to contemporary standards; it does not in fact require someone in fact saw the act and was outraged. In most cases, there will be no evidence against a defendant unless the act is seen by someone; but that does not mean that where an act is in fact done which is lewd, obscene or disgusting and is of a nature that outrages public decency and is done where it is proved that people are present and capable of seeing its nature, it is not an offence.[74]

Fault element

3.39 Outraging public decency is generally said to be an offence of strict liability. That is, it need not include any intention to disgust or to be indecent. The same has been held in connection with other offences in which indecency or public offence is a factor: for example conspiracy to corrupt public morals[75] and blasphemous libel.[76] Conversely, an act is not an offence if it was performed with a sexually improper motive but was not objectively indecent in itself, as in *Rowley*,[77] where the defendant left a series of notes to boys inviting them to meet him: the notes had no improper content but the defendant clearly had sexual designs.

3.40 The question was discussed fully in *Gibson and Sylveire*.[78] After considering the cases, in particular the nineteenth-century nude bathing cases[79] and those concerning other offences such as blasphemous or obscene libel and the statutory predecessors of the Obscene Publication Acts,[80] all of which indicated that intention to shock was not an ingredient of the offences in question, the court concluded that:

> ... where the charge is one of outraging public decency, there is no requirement that the prosecution should prove an intention to outrage or such recklessness as is submitted by Mr Robertson. If the publication takes place, and if it is deliberate, there is, in the words of Lord Russell:[81] "no justification for holding that there is no offence

---

[73] 1 Cox CC 74.

[74] *Hamilton* para 39.

[75] *Shaw v DPP* [1962] AC 220.

[76] *Whitehouse v Gay News Ltd* [1979] AC 617 (also known as *Lemon*).

[77] [1991] 1 WLR 1020, [1991] 4 All ER 649, 94 Cr App R 95 (CA).

[78] [1990] 2 QB 619.

[79] *Crunden* (1809) 2 Camp 89; *Reed* (1871) 12 Cox CC 1.

[80] *Hicklin* (1868) LR 3 QB 360.

[81] *Gay News* case [1979] AC 617, 657-658.

when the publisher is incapable for some reason particular to himself of agreeing with the jury on the true nature of the publication."[82]

3.41   It seems that outraging public decency is also an offence of strict liability as to the requirement of being in public: it is not necessary that the defendant knew or believed that the act or object was likely to be seen at all, let alone to disgust. In *Rose v DPP* the defendant was totally oblivious of the presence of a CCTV camera, and while his appeal was allowed this was on other grounds. Similarly in *Hamilton* the defendant was found guilty although, far from intending to create a spectacle, he was clearly counting on not being seen.

3.42   On the other hand, the offence requires intention to perform the physical act in question, just as criminal libel required intention to publish. Lord Lane CJ in *Gibson and Sylveire* summarised the prosecution submissions (which he accepted) as follows:

> ... the object of the common law offence is to protect the public from suffering feelings of outrage by such exhibition. Thus, if a defendant *intentionally* does an act which *in fact* outrages public decency (our italics), the public will suffer outrage whatever the defendant's state of mind may be. If the defendant's state of mind is a critical factor, then, he submits, a man could escape liability by the very baseness of his own standards.[83]

On this reasoning, the offence does not cover the case of a person who exposes himself inadvertently because his clothes were torn in an accident.

OTHER COUNTRIES

Australia

3.43   In New South Wales[84] and Victoria, which have partial criminal codes but retain the concept of common law offences, outraging public decency appears to be a common law offence as in England and Wales.[85] In states with full criminal codes, various definitions appear: a typical example is Queensland, where the Criminal Code 1899 provides:

> **227. Indecent acts**
>
> (1) Any person who--
>
> > (a) wilfully and without lawful excuse does any indecent act in any place to which the public are permitted to have access, whether on payment of a charge for admission or not; or

---

[82]   [1990] 2 QB 619, 629.

[83]   [1990] 2 QB 619, 627.

[84]   http://www.findlaw.com.au/article/12642.htm. Outraging public decency is mentioned in *Bodyline Spa & Sauna (Sydney) Pty Ltd v South Sidney City Council* (1992) 77 LGRA 432 as an ingredient of the offence of keeping a disorderly house. See also the New South Wales Law Reform Commission Discussion Paper 24 (1992) – Blasphemy, para 4.38.

[85]   For example, the Australian Law Journal thought it worth noting the case of *Hamilton*: (2008) 82 ALJ 316.

(b) wilfully does any indecent act in any place with intent to insult or offend any person;

is guilty of a misdemeanour, and is liable to imprisonment for 2 years.

(2) The offender may be arrested without warrant.

(3) Subsection (1) does not apply to a person who does an indecent act under the authority of an adult entertainment permit.

Canada

3.44   The Canadian Criminal Code provides:

173.—(1)   Every one who wilfully does an indecent act

(a) in a public place in the presence of one or more persons, or

(b) in any place, with intent thereby to insult or offend any person,

is guilty of an offence punishable on summary conviction.

(2) Every person who, in any place, for a sexual purpose, exposes his or her genital organs to a person who is under the age of fourteen years is guilty of an offence punishable on summary conviction.

174.—(1)   Every one who, without lawful excuse,

(a) is nude in a public place, or

(b) is nude and exposed to public view while on private property, whether or not the property is his own,

is guilty of an offence punishable on summary conviction.

(2) For purposes of this section, a person is nude who is so clad as to offend against public decency or order.

(3) No proceedings shall be commenced under this section without the consent of the Attorney General.

3.45   Other offences in the Criminal Code that contain the concept of indecency are:

(1)   section 163(2)(b): publicly exhibiting an indecent show;

(2)   section 167: indecent theatrical performance;

(3)   section 168: mailing indecent matter;

(4)   section 175(1)(b): causing disturbance by indecent exhibition;

(5)   section 197: definition of common bawdy house includes a place resorted to for the practice of acts of indecency.

New Zealand

3.46   The Crimes Act 1961 provides:

124. Distribution or exhibition of indecent matter

(1) Every one is liable to imprisonment for a term not exceeding 2 years who, without lawful justification or excuse,—

  (a) sells, exposes for sale, or otherwise distributes to the public any indecent model or object; or

  (b) exhibits or presents in or within view of any place to which the public have or are permitted to have access any indecent object or indecent show or performance; or

  (c) exhibits or presents in the presence of any person in consideration or expectation of any payment or otherwise for gain, any indecent show or performance.

(2) It is a defence to a charge under this section to prove that the public good was served by the acts alleged to have been done.

(3) It is a question of law whether the sale, exposure for sale, distribution, exhibition, or presentation might in the circumstances serve the public good, and whether there is evidence of excess beyond what the public good requires; but it is a question of fact whether or not the acts complained of did so serve the public good and whether or not there was such excess.

(4) It is no defence that the person charged did not know that the model, object, show, or performance to which the charge relates was indecent, unless that person also satisfies the court—

  (a) that he had no reasonable opportunity of knowing it; and

  (b) that in the circumstances his ignorance was excusable.

(5) No one shall be prosecuted for an offence against this section without the leave of the Attorney-General, who before giving leave may make such inquiries as he thinks fit.

(6) Nothing in this section shall apply to any publication within the meaning of the Films, Videos, and Publications Classification Act 1993, whether the publication is objectionable within the meaning of that Act or not.

125. Indecent act in public place

(1) Every one is liable to imprisonment for a term not exceeding 2 years who wilfully does any indecent act in any place to which the public have or are permitted to have access, or within view of any such place.

(2) It is a defence to a charge under this section if the person charged proves that he had reasonable grounds for believing that he would not be observed.

(3) For the purposes of this section, the term place includes any railway carriage, and also includes any ship, aircraft, or vehicle used for the carriage of passengers for hire or reward.

126. Indecent act with intent to insult or offend

Every one is liable to imprisonment for a term not exceeding 2 years who with intent to insult or offend any person does any indecent act in any place.

PART 4
CRITICISMS AND PROPOSALS: THE CONDUCT ELEMENT

PUBLIC NUISANCE

Abolishing the offence

4.1 Arguments for abolishing the offence of public nuisance, as advanced by Spencer, fall under the following heads.

(1) Vagueness of definition.

(2) Incompatibility with the constitutional requirement of the rule of law.

(3) Problems of compatibility with the European Convention on Human Rights.

(4) Redundancy, as having been superseded by statutory nuisance and other modern statutory offences and mechanisms.

Vagueness of definition

4.2 Spencer argues that, historically, the factual element of public nuisance was extremely fluid and virtually indistinguishable from the now defunct offence of public mischief,[1] and that both offences could be extended to criminalise anything the judges disliked. Such freedom of judicial law-making is not acceptable in a modern democracy.[2]

4.3 In *Rimmington*[3] it was acknowledged that this criticism would have force if the offence was interpreted so widely as to cover unlocalised and individually focused mischiefs such as the making of obscene telephone calls or the sending of hate mail (as in the actual case), whatever the cumulative public effect. A series of authorities suggesting that these were public nuisances was therefore overruled.[4] The House of Lords accepted that this wide interpretation of the offence was tantamount to reviving the offence of public mischief.[5]

4.4 However, they clearly did not accept Spencer's argument[6] that the overall definition of the offence was so platitudinous as not to be a definition at all, so that there was no certainty in relation to any branch of the offence. On the contrary, Lord Bingham observed:[7]

---

[1] Held not to exist by the House of Lords in *DPP v Withers* [1975] AC 842.

[2] [1989] CLJ 55 at pp 78-9.

[3] [2006] 1 AC 459 (HL).

[4] *Rimmington*, paras 23 to 27, 37, 46 to 48: see paras 2.26 and 2.27 above.

[5] Spencer pp 62, 79; *Rimmington* para 37.

[6] At pp 65-66.

[7] *Rimmington*, para 36; see para 2.17 above.

I would for my part accept that the offence as defined by Stephen, as defined in *Archbold* (save for the reference to morals), as enacted in the Commonwealth codes quoted above and as applied in the cases … referred to in paras 13 to 22 above is clear, precise, adequately defined and based on a discernible rational principle. A legal adviser asked to give his opinion in advance would ascertain whether the act or omission contemplated was likely to inflict significant injury on a substantial section of the public exercising their ordinary rights as such: if so, an obvious risk of causing a public nuisance would be apparent; if not, not.

4.5   For our part, we accept that the offence, as developed through the cases up to and including *Rimmington*, has reached a reasonable degree of certainty. However, we do not believe that this certainty is derived from, or expressed in, verbal definitions such as the ones in Stephen and *Archbold*. Rather, it may be found in the historical distinction, expressed above,[8] between "core" nuisance with a clear analogy with private nuisance (the first category) and the miscellaneous forms of misbehaviour classified with it (the second category). The actual decision in *Rimmington* may be paraphrased by saying that, even in nuisances of the second category, the definitions must be read subject to the further unexpressed requirement that the link with "core" nuisance (the "intellectual moorings"[9]) must not be too remote. It remains the case that nuisance must be defined piecemeal, as similar to nuisances that have been found in the past. The European Court of Human Rights has affirmed the legitimacy of such an exercise, when undertaken by the courts.[10]

4.6   It is the second category that largely underlies Spencer's complaint of formlessness and extensibility. This category is cut down by *Rimmington* with the result that the practical application, if not the intellectual force, of that complaint is significantly reduced.

4.7   By the same token, however, the offence may have lost some of its attractiveness to prosecutors, who are said to find it convenient, both to cover varieties of anti-social behaviour not quite caught by specific statutory offences and as a stronger offence in instances where the statutory offence has strict time limits or limited sentencing powers that are not appropriate to the gravity of what occurred.[11] This convenience would have been still stronger in the broad form of the offence as it existed before *Rimmington*; but this breadth is something of a luxury, and if one were setting out to devise a criminal code it would be difficult, and probably undesirable in principle, to draft an offence of similar generality.

---

[8]   Para 2.11.

[9]   *Rimmington* para 37.

[10]   *SW & CR v UK* (1995) 21 EHRR 363.

[11]   According to Spencer, pp 77-78, cited in *Rimmington*, para 37.

Rule of law

4.8 Lord Bingham devotes a lengthy passage[12] to considering Bentham's criticism of retrospective judicial legislation ("dog law", or "law following the event"), and observes that:

> The domestic law of England and Wales has set its face firmly against "dog-law". In *R v Withers*[13] the House of Lords ruled that the judges have no power to create new offences: see Lord Reid, at p 854g; Viscount Dilhorne, at p 860e; Lord Simon of Glaisdale, at pp 863d, 867e; Lord Kilbrandon, at p 877c. Nor (per Lord Simon, at p 863d) may the courts nowadays widen existing offences so as to make punishable conduct of a type hitherto not subject to punishment.

He further refers to this doctrine as "these common law principles".[14]

4.9 In its original context, Bentham's criticism was probably meant as an attack on the existence of common law as such rather than as a caution against excessive judicial activism in the field of criminal law. Nevertheless neither Lord Bingham nor Judge LJ whom he cites denied the legitimacy of common law offences as such. Their point was that the court may not *now* create new offences: the caution against judicial law-making is not itself retrospective. Public mischief is objectionable, not because it is in origin a judge-made offence, but because it is so vague in outline that every instance of it is an occasion for fresh judicial law-making.

4.10 In Lord Bingham's analysis, Bentham's "dog law" argument, against retrospective judicial legislation, cuts both ways. One cannot indefinitely extend a common law offence to include everything which one dislikes as a matter of policy. But by the same token one cannot hold that, as the offence is now unnecessary, it should be treated as never having existed. At most, one can make incremental extensions or prunings designed to bring the offence nearer to the logical boundaries implicit in its original nature and purpose.

> It may very well be, as suggested by J R Spencer in his article cited in para 6 above, at p 83, that "There is surely a strong case for abolishing the crime of public nuisance". But as the courts have no power to create new offences (see para 33 below), so they have no power to abolish existing offences. That is a task for Parliament, following careful consideration (perhaps undertaken, in the first instance, by the Law Commission) whether there are aspects of the public interest which the crime of public nuisance has a continuing role to protect. It is not in my view open to the House in resolving these appeals to conclude that the common law crime of causing a public nuisance no longer exists.[15]

---

[12] *Rimmington* para 33.

[13] [1975] AC 842.

[14] *Rimmington* para 34.

[15] *Rimmington* para 31.

Human rights

4.11   One of the questions raised in *Rimmington* was the compatibility of the offence of public nuisance with the European Convention on Human Rights. The main article engaged was Article 7:

> No one shall be held guilty of any criminal offence on account of any act or omission which did not constitute a criminal offence under national or international law at the time when it was committed. Nor shall a heavier penalty be imposed than the one that was applicable at the time the criminal offence was committed.

Other relevant articles were Articles 8 and 10, concerning respect for correspondence and freedom of expression.

4.12   The Court of Appeal, upholding the convictions, held that the law of public nuisance was formulated with sufficient precision to enable a citizen to regulate his conduct, and that the interference with correspondence and freedom of expression was a proper and proportionate response to the need to protect the public.

4.13   Andrew Ashworth, in his commentary on the Court of Appeal's decision,[16] cast some doubt on both these conclusions. Public nuisance, as then formulated, was such a broad, catch-all offence that it arguably did not have the necessary certainty. Also, by carrying an unlimited power of sentencing it might well not be "proportionate"; while the uncertainty of the definition meant that the interference with Article 8 and 10 rights was not "in accordance with the law". Further, given the wide range of public nuisance the issue of proportionality would need to be assessed afresh in each case. It was legitimate to extend the scope of offences, but only on a step by step basis and in such a way that the extended scope was reasonably foreseeable to the accused's legal advisers.[17] He expressed the hope that the House of Lords would reassert the principles of the rule of law by insisting on greater certainty of definition. He accepted that the major reassessment of public nuisance and other common law offences needed to be done by law reformers and the legislature rather than by the courts.

4.14   The House of Lords reaffirmed that from the point of view of human rights and of the rule of law, there is no objection in principle to the existence of common law offences,[18] provided that they can be defined with reasonable (not absolute) certainty. This allows for the sort of foreseeable, incremental change that follows from the original concept of the offence. Public nuisance, leaving aside for the moment the *Norbury* and *Johnson* line of authority,[19] satisfies this test.[20]

---

[16]   [2004] Crim LR 304.

[17]   In *SW & CR v UK* (1995) 21 EHRR 363 (concerning marital rape) the European Court held that judicial extensions of the criminal law can be justified if they could reasonably have been foreseen as arising from the original scope of the offence.

[18]   *Rimmington*, para 35.

[19]   Para 2.26 above.

[20]   *Rimmington*, para 36. See further *SW & CR v UK* (above).

4.15   However, as we have seen, the extension of the offence by *Norbury* and *Johnson* to include activities such as obscene telephone calls and hate mail was held not to be in accordance with the internal logic of the offence or to follow from its original concept.[21] For that reason it also fell foul of the rule of law and the Convention requirements. The House of Lords did not address the Article 8 or 10 point in detail, though they alluded to the "in accordance with the law" test:[22] on the view they took of the law the question did not arise, as the *Norbury/Johnson* extension had already fallen at the Article 7 hurdle.

4.16   It is important to note that the House of Lords in *Rimmington* was concerned not with the question of whether public nuisance should exist and what its boundaries should be in an ideal world but with how far they could be rationalised within the existing authorities. Once objections of a constitutional character, such as human rights and the rule of law, are found to be ungrounded, that exhausts any judicial capacity to hold that an offence does not exist, but that is without prejudice to the policy question of whether it should be abolished by the legislature. They therefore left open the possibility that the Law Commission, or the legislature, might wish for a more radical reform, on the lines suggested by Spencer.

4.17   Nevertheless, we consider that their conclusions are equally valid when transposed to the context of law reform, even though they were not intended for that purpose. If the offence is certain enough not to fall foul of considerations of human rights and the rule of law, that is also an answer to any policy objection on the grounds of vagueness.

Overlap with other offences

4.18   Another point made by Spencer is that the offence of public nuisance is now unnecessary as most instances are covered by specialised statutory offences. This is also discussed in *Rimmington*.[23] The House of Lords acknowledged that most instances of public nuisance are now covered by specialised statutory offences,[24] and that it is preferable to use these where possible.[25] It does not follow from this that the law of public nuisance is now a dead letter and that the offence has ceased to exist, or even that it cannot lawfully be used when a statutory offence is available.[26]

4.19   It is true that most instances of public nuisance within the environmental category are covered either by statutory nuisance under the Environmental Protection Act 1990 or by other specialised offences. The penalties for these are limited, and the mechanisms are mostly aimed at incidental nuisances caused in the course of a bona fide business, which are properly addressed by a compliance strategy. There remain the instances of flagrant and wilful environmental nuisance for which the statutory sanctions are inadequate and where the prosecution may

---

[21] *Rimmington*, para 37, set out in full at para 2.27 above.

[22] *Rimmington*, para 34.

[23] *Rimmington*, para 30.

[24] *Rimmington*, para 29.

[25] *Rimmington*, para 30.

[26] *Rimmington*, para 30.

quite properly, in Spencer's words, want "a bigger or extra stick to beat him with".[27] This may however be an argument for strengthening the fault element of the offence so that only these more serious cases are covered.

4.20 One example where this use of public nuisance was legitimate and useful was *Bourgass*,[28] concerning a person who compiled recipes and collected materials for the manufacture of ricin and cyanide in circumstances indicating an intention to use them in terrorist activities. The appeal was partly against sentence and partly on the question of fair trial: the merits of the choice of public nuisance as an offence were not discussed. In the current climate public reaction to the abolition without replacement of a broad-based offence addressing this type of behaviour is unlikely to be favourable.

4.21 Similarly we are not convinced that the behavioural side of the offence is unnecessary because its scope (even as limited by *Rimmington*) is exhausted by statutory offences. It is highly likely that there will always be a public interest in maintaining an offence that covers analogous kinds of case, if only as a stop-gap as the legislature endeavours to keep pace. That does not justify a general offence of doing anything which there is reason to dislike. On the other hand, it is not clear that a broad offence, of which the generic outlines are reasonably clear, is always adequately replaceable by a series of offences listing each particular permutation in laborious detail.[29] As stated in *Rimmington*,[30] in connection with the Strasbourg human rights jurisprudence:

> It is accepted that absolute certainty is unattainable, and might entail excessive rigidity since the law must be able to keep pace with changing circumstances, some degree of vagueness is inevitable and development of the law is a recognised feature of common law courts.[31]

Conclusion on abolition or retention of the offence

4.22 Prosecutors, both local authorities and the Crown Prosecution Service, do not make extensive use of public nuisance as a common law offence, preferring to reserve it for extreme and wilful instances of misbehaviour. In answer to questions from the Law Commission they have indicated that they wish to keep this weapon in their armoury, as the statutory offences and mechanisms are not always adequate, either in breadth or in gravity, for misbehaviour of this kind. We are inclined to agree that public nuisance still has a role to play in these cases.

4.23 The convenience of prosecutors would not be a sufficient reason to retain the offence if it were found to contravene the principles of human rights and the rule of law or fell short of minimum standards of legal certainty, as argued by Spencer. As argued above, however, following *Rimmington* public nuisance

---

[27] Spencer, p 77, cited at *Rimmington*, para 37.

[28] [2006] EWCA Crim 3397.

[29] For this argument, see the extract from Lord Simon's speech in *Knuller*, para 3.5 above.

[30] *Rimmington*, para 35.

[31] *Sunday Times v United Kingdom* 2 EHRR 245, para 49; *X Ltd and Y v United Kingdom* (1982) 28 DR 77, 81, para 9; *SW v United Kingdom* 21 EHRR 363, para 36/34 (footnote in judgment).

does not offend against those principles and standards. We therefore consider that the offence should be retained.

Reforming the conduct element

4.24   We agree with the House of Lords in *Rimmington* that it is not desirable either to limit the definition of public nuisance so as to exclude all instances falling within other offences or to lay down that, where another offence is applicable, prosecuting for public nuisance is always an abuse of process. Formal exclusions to prevent overlap with statutory offences are often problematic, a case in point being conspiracy to defraud between 1977 and 1987.[32]

4.25   In the 1879 draft Criminal Code,[33] and in the criminal code of Canada,[34] there is a two-step test for public nuisance; while the existence of public nuisance is defined in much the same way as in England and Wales, it is not made criminal unless it endangers life, safety or health or causes an injury. The criminal code of New Zealand reaches a similar result by requiring danger to life, safety or health as part of the basic definition.[35]

4.26   We are not aware of any proposal that the scope of public nuisance in England and Wales should be limited in the same way, except for Spencer's suggestion that public nuisance should be replaced by an offence of doing anything which creates a major hazard to the physical safety or health of the public. This definition might prove to be unduly restrictive: there is still room for an offence of wilful conduct causing a major loss of amenity as distinct from a threat to health and safety. There is even a case for saying that this is the more important of the two, as health and safety risks are more comprehensively covered by specialised legislation.

4.27   **We provisionally propose that the offence of public nuisance be retained, and that its conduct element should remain in its present form as laid down in *Rimmington*.**

OUTRAGING PUBLIC DECENCY

Abolishing the offence

4.28   Outraging public decency has not been the object of an all-out attack similar to Spencer's criticism of public nuisance. Nevertheless it can be considered under the same heads, namely certainty/human rights/rule of law, overlap with statutory offences and reform of the conduct element. (Reform of the fault element and codification are considered in Part 5 and Part 6.)

---

[32]   *Ayres* [1984] AC 447. The result was reversed by Criminal Justice Act 1987 s 12(1). Between 1984 and 1987, the Inland Revenue was unable to prosecute for conspiracy to defraud, as the possibility existed of prosecuting for a statutory conspiracy to commit the near-obsolete common law offence of cheating, applicable only to Revenue cases.

[33]   Para 2.32.

[34]   Para 2.64.

[35]   Para 2.62.

Human rights and the rule of law

4.29 Following the decision in *Gibson and Sylveire* both defendants applied to the European Human Rights Commission in Strasbourg,[36] claiming that their conviction was a breach of their right to freedom of expression under Article 10 of the European Convention on Human Rights. The Commission did not allow their application to proceed further, holding that the restriction was sufficiently "prescribed by law" and pursued a "legitimate aim", namely the protection of morality, by means falling within the permissible margin of appreciation.

4.30 *Smith and Hogan* comments that:

> Despite the recent efforts of the courts to clarify the *actus reus* elements in *Hamilton* and *Rose* it remains doubtful whether the offence is sufficiently certain to be prescribed by law within Art 10, or necessary and proportionate within Art 10(2). There is clearly scope for reform of this offence by Parliament.[37]

4.31 This decision is also criticised by Tom Lewis.[38] He argues, first, that the type of conduct falling within the offence is not sufficiently certain and, secondly, that the protection of the public from shock or outrage is, in *Knuller*, expressly differentiated from the protection of morals and cannot now be defended as an instance of it.[39]

4.32 We do not agree with the first argument. If an offence is defined as consisting of any conduct which produces a given result, and the result is defined with sufficient certainty, the definition of the offence does not become unacceptably uncertain because of purely factual doubts as to whether a given course of conduct will produce that result. The kind and degree of adverse public reaction is sufficiently defined in the cases up to and including *Knuller*, *Gibson* and *Hamilton*. Under our proposals, conduct will only be criminal if it is foreseen as liable to produce that reaction: if (which we do not believe) the offence as at present defined is too vague to be useful as a guide to conduct, this will no longer be the case if our proposals are implemented. By confining the offence to deliberate or reckless conduct, the proposals should also meet any objection on the ground of proportionality.

4.33 The second argument has more substance, and we are inclined to agree that the justification for the offence in cases like *Gibson* is not to do with the protection of morals. The object of the offence, as explained by Lord Simon in *Knuller*, is "that reasonable people should be able to venture into public without their sense of decency being outraged".[40] This in our opinion falls within the exception for "the protection of the reputation or rights of others" in Article 10(2) of the Convention.

---

[36] *S and G v UK* App No 17634/91.

[37] Para 31.3.14.3 (p 1059).

[38] "Human Earrings, Human Rights and Public Decency", Entertainment Law, Vol.1, No.2, Summer 2002, p 50.

[39] A further point is that if, in publication cases such as *Knuller*, the restriction were held to exist for the protection of morals, then the publication would fall under OPA 1959 s 2(4), and be chargeable only under the Obscene Publications Act and not as a common law offence.

[40] [1973] AC 435, 493, cited with agreement in *Hamilton* para 36.

Like other offences with an environmental flavour, outraging public decency exists to protect a right to public amenity. If for example an artistic installation had the effect of blocking the public highway for several hours, or filling a residential neighbourhood with a malodorous vapour or with noise on an industrial scale, it would clearly fall within the offence of public nuisance and could not be defended as the exercise of freedom of artistic expression. The same must in principle be true of indecent public displays, if indecent enough.

4.34 We are not concerned here with the correctness of *Gibson*, so far as that depends on whether the degree of offensiveness on the facts of that case was sufficient to trigger the public's right to protection, and Lewis may be right to criticise that particular prosecution as a steam-hammer to crack a nut. We do however consider that the human rights argument cannot be used to impugn the existence of the offence of outraging public decency or its application to artistic expression, even if it can be used to impugn particular decisions to prosecute as being disproportionate.

Overlap with other offences

4.35 Many instances of this offence now fall within various statutory offences, such as those against:

    (1)   section 66 of the Sexual Offences Act 2003 (exposure);

    (2)   the Obscene Publications Acts;

    (3)   section 2 of the Theatres Act 1968;

    (4)   the Indecent Displays (Control) Act 1981;

    (5)   section 4 of the Metropolitan Police Act 1839;

    (6)   the Children and Young Persons (Harmful Publications) Act 1955.

As with public nuisance, however, the cases show that the scope of human inventiveness is infinite and that there is still the need for a broadly based offence covering the varieties of public indecency.

4.36 Prosecutors inform us that, in several respects, the common law offence is more convenient in practice than the statutory offence of exposure, and that it is the only offence available for cases such as *Hamilton*. The current number of prosecutions is 300-400 per year.[41]

Reforming the conduct element

4.37 There is nothing obviously unreasonable about the factual scope of the offence, and following *Rose v DPP* and *Hamilton* its outlines are reasonably clear. In particular, as with public nuisance the focus has been clarified:[42] the offence is designed to protect the public from witnessing disgusting sights and sounds, and is not a catch-all tool for the enforcement of morality.

---

[41] Figure supplied by Crown Prosecution Service.

[42] Paras 3.11, 3.23, 3.26 above.

4.38   The main issue in *Hamilton* was whether there is any necessity for the act to be actually seen by a member of the public. *Smith and Hogan*[43] comments:

> Controversially, the court declined to restrict the offence so as to require *actual* sight or sound of the nature of the act. ... The Court of Appeal accepted that all the reported cases had involved one person *being present* seeing the act, but held that the requirement of present case (sic) a matter of evidence rather than one of substantive law. This is a very surprising conclusion. It demonstrates a willingness to extend the common law to tackle new mischief which the House of Lords had deprecated in *Rimmington* in the context of public nuisance.[44]

4.39   This is not so much a criticism of the result as of the process by which it was reached. From the point of view of law reform, it is not at all clear that the offence would be the better for a requirement that a person actually see the acts in question without necessarily being disgusted by them. We agree with the Court of Appeal that such a requirement adds nothing either to the element of undesirable publicity or to the element of indecency.

4.40   It could be argued that *Hamilton*, though right in its result, was right for the wrong reason.[45] The real harm of the defendant's actions consisted not in the possibility that one of the women would notice and feel humiliated, or that another passer-by would notice and feel indignation, but rather in the fact that even if there was no possibility of discovery it is an unacceptable invasion of privacy. The offensiveness was in seeing, rather than (potentially) being seen, and the act should therefore fall within a separate offence of voyeurism rather than one basically concerned with exhibitionism. Unfortunately it did not quite fall within the voyeurism offence created by section 67 of the Sexual Offences Act 2003, and was in any case committed before that offence came into force.[46] Outraging public decency was therefore used as a stop-gap.

4.41   That may be a reason to reform the Sexual Offences Act. It is not a reason to reform the offence of outraging public decency, as the potential harm targeted by that offence was certainly present in *Hamilton*, even if, as argued above, it is not the most important fact about it.

Provisional proposal

4.42   These arguments are sufficient to persuade us that there is no *obvious* case for abolishing the offence or radically altering its conduct element, within the limits of a simplification project.[47] It may be that a more wide-ranging and fundamental review would lead to a different view of where the offence should fit in among the wider spectrum of indecency-related offences: for example, a different rationale could be provided for penalising voyeuristic acts like those in *Hamilton*.

---

[43]   Para 31.3.14.1 (p 1058).

[44]   Italics in original.

[45]   For a criticism of this use of the offence, see Gillespie, "Upskirts and Down Blouses" [2008] Crim LR 370; cited *Smith and Hogan* p 1058 n 302.

[46]   *Hamilton* para 28.

4.43 **We provisionally propose that the offence of outraging public decency be retained, and that its conduct element should remain in its present form as laid down in *Hamilton*.**

---

[47] Para 1.4 above.

PART 5
CRITICISMS AND PROPOSALS: THE FAULT ELEMENT

5.1 In this Part, we make the case for provisionally proposing that the fault element, both for public nuisance and for outraging public decency, should be *intention or recklessness*. The prosecution should have to show *either*

(1) that D intended to cause a public nuisance, or to outrage public decency, *or*

(2) if that cannot be shown, that D was reckless as to whether his or her conduct would cause a public nuisance, or outrage public decency.

So far as the latter possibility is concerned, what must be shown is that D was aware that his or her conduct might cause a public nuisance, or lead to public decency being outraged, and yet unjustifiably went on to take the risk of that happening.[1]

OFFENCES IN GENERAL AND FAULT REQUIREMENTS

5.2 Fault elements attached to criminal offences vary very considerably, both at common law and in statute. It has been argued that this in itself blights the system as a whole, and that greater narrowness of focus and uniformity should be brought to the treatment of fault in English criminal law as a whole. For example, in an earlier edition of their work Smith and Hogan argued (approving of English law as they believed that it stood before the decision in *Caldwell*[2]) that:

> Before *Caldwell* it could be said that…in crimes requiring *mens rea*, as distinct from negligence, intention or recklessness as to all the elements of the offence was *mens rea* or the basic constituent of it.[3]

5.3 Even if this was the 'pre-*Caldwell*' position (which, with respect, we doubt), it trades for its plausibility on an ambiguity in the notion of '*mens rea*'. If '*mens rea*' means 'mental' element then Smith and Hogan's claim has, perhaps, some degree of plausibility; but if '*mens rea*' means, as we will take it to mean, 'fault' element, then Smith and Hogan's claim cannot be substantiated. It has long been understood that 'negligence' is a kind of fault element.[4] Not only can homicide be committed by (gross) negligence, but there is also a negligence basis to liability in rape, even though rape is a very serious crime respecting which great stigma follows conviction.[5] Further, few now argue for subjective recklessness to be re-

---

[1] We mean here to invoke the authoritative understanding of recklessness given in *G* [2003] UKHL 50, [2004] 1 AC 1034.

[2] [1982] AC 341.

[3] Smith and Hogan, *Criminal Law* (7th ed, 1992) at p 70.

[4] For a recent discussion, see AP Simester, 'Can Negligence be Culpable?', in Jeremy Horder (ed) *Oxford Essays in Jurisprudence*, 4th Series (2000).

[5] See now the Sexual Offences Act 2003 s 1.

instated as the fault element in what is now the offence of 'dangerous driving', even though conviction for that crime too carries considerable stigma.[6]

5.4 Having said that, there is a still a strong case for saying that the same or very similar fault requirements should be employed where two or more of the following criteria are met:

> The offences are of a broadly similar nature;

> The offences are at about the same level of gravity; and

> The offences may in many instances interchangeably be charged on the same facts.

5.5 This is in a way a very simple and easily met demand. If met, it means, so far as the fault element is concerned, that differences of definition where there need be none have been avoided, making the law easier to understand for all concerned. It also makes choice of charge a more straightforward matter for the prosecution, by enabling a concentration of focus on how well the facts fit the conduct element of a given crime, in determining whether there is a reasonable prospect of conviction.

5.6 This is where *Smith and Hogan*'s focus on intention or recklessness, as key fault terms in criminal law, can still have an important bearing. There are a number of offences broadly comparable to public nuisance and outraging public decency in point of gravity. For these offences, the fault element is either intention or recklessness (or malice or awareness) as to the occurrence of the conduct elements (even if fault is not required respecting all the elements[7]), as recommended by *Smith and Hogan* in 1992.[8]

5.7 In that regard, the definition of intention is now settled by the case of *Woollin*.[9] In law, intention involves a desire to bring something about, a desire which may be inferred from proof that the person in question foresaw that the event in question was virtually certain to come about if they acted in a certain way (which they went on to do).

5.8 Recklessness, in law, now follows the meaning set out in the Draft Criminal Code:

> A person acts recklessly ... with respect to —

> (i) a circumstance when he is aware of a risk that it exists or will exist;

> (ii) a result when he is aware of a risk that it will occur;

---

[6] Even if the concept of 'dangerous' driving is, for some, less acceptable than a standard that can take greater account of blameworthiness, such as 'negligent' driving. For a comprehensive review of driving offences involving the causing of death, see Sally Cunningham, 'Punishing Drivers who Kill: Putting Road Safety First'? (2007) 27 *Legal Studies* 288.

[7] See paras 5.24 and following, below.

[8] Above, n 3.

[9] [1999] 1 AC 82 (HL).

(iii) and it is, in the circumstances known to him, unreasonable to take the risk.[10]

PARTICULAR OFFENCES WITH SIMILAR FAULT ELEMENTS

Some analogous offences

5.9 Examples of crimes that exactly or closely follow these fault requirements – intention and recklessness (including words broadly equivalent to recklessness, such as 'malice' or 'awareness') - include criminal damage, some offences against the person, and some public order offences.

5.10 Examples of offences with a requirement for proof of intention or recklessness are as follows.

(1) Criminal damage.[11]

(2) Assault occasioning actual bodily harm.[12]

(3) Assault at common law.

5.11 Examples of offences where intention or 'awareness' of risk is sufficient are as follows:

(1) Riot.[13]

(2) Violent disorder.[14]

(3) Affray.[15]

(4) Threatening, abusive or insulting words or behaviour.[16]

5.12 Examples of offences where 'malice' (meaning intention or recklessness) is sufficient, are as follows:

(1) Malicious infliction of grievous bodily harm.[17]

(2) Maliciously administering a destructive or noxious thing.[18]

---

[10] This definition was adopted by Lord Bingham in *G* [2003] UKHL 50, [2004] 1 AC 1034.

[11] Criminal Damage Act 1971 s 1(1). See *G*, above.

[12] Offences Against the Person Act 1861 s 47.

[13] Public Order Act s 1. In relation to riot, *Smith and Hogan*, para 32.1.3.5 (p 1066), says: "It must be proved that a person charged with riot shared that common purpose and that he (but not necessarily the other 11 or more) intended to use violence or was aware that his conduct might be violent, and it is important that this is made clear to the jury."

[14] POA 1986 s 2.

[15] POA 1986 s 3.

[16] POA 1986 s 4.

[17] OAPA 1861 s 20.

[18] OAPA 1861 s 23.

5.13   We do not regard the difference between 'recklessness,' 'awareness' and 'malice' as of any special significance in this context.[19]

How the offences cover similar ground

5.14   We have chosen the offences mentioned above because it is realistic to suppose that one or other of public nuisance, and outraging public decency, may fall to be prosecuted on similar or not dissimilar facts. For example:

> D's job involves stacking supermarket shelves. D, in view of his fellow workers, urinates on vegetables before putting them out on display.

5.15   In this example, it would be possible to charge D with criminal damage to the vegetables. However, a charge of outraging public decency seems just as likely or appropriate; perhaps more so.

5.16   Here is another example:

> D bears a striking resemblance to a well-known terrorist. He regularly dons a large overcoat to make it look as if he might have a home-made bomb attached to his body. He then goes out into the street and rushes right up to individual people with his arms outstretched. His actions often cause those people, and others around them, to panic.

5.17   In this example, D could be charged with assaulting each person, by putting them in fear of the application of violence. D could also be charged with having engaged in threatening behaviour.[20] However, a charge of public nuisance might be just as appropriate, given that it reflects the continued nature of D's offending behaviour.[21]

5.18   Here is a further example:

> D prints notices with racially inflammatory messages in large print on them. D then sticks them to the clothes or possessions of members of ethnic minorities as they go about their business, whenever D can do so without the individual in question noticing.

5.19   In this example, D could perhaps be charged with, amongst other possibilities, insulting behaviour, contrary to the Public Order Act 1986.[22] However, a charge of public nuisance might be as or more appropriate.

5.20   Here is a final example:

> D advertises in local shops and newspapers that there will be a "£20,000 giveaway" at particular times on particular days in the local

---

[19] For further discussion, see *Smith and Hogan* para 32.1.3.5 (p 1066). See para 5.51 below for the application of the distinction to outraging public decency.

[20] Public Order Act 1986 s 5(1).

[21] On these facts, D's conduct probably falls outside the scope of the Criminal Law Act 1977 s 51 (bomb hoaxes).

[22] See para 5.11(4).

market square, when he will throw that sum of money in £50 notes from the balcony of the town hall. On some occasions, no public disturbance is caused when D throws the money to the ground as promised, but on one occasion a large crowd gathered and an affray ensued as people fought to grab the £50 notes.

5.21 In this example, it is possible that D could be charged with affray, in so far as he procures one. It might be equally or more appropriate to charge D with public nuisance.

The fault element in the analogous offences: strict and constructive liability

5.22 Conspicuously, the offences analogous to public nuisance and outraging public decency cannot be committed when the conduct element takes place only through negligence (through inadvertence) on the part of the defendant. As we shall argue below,[23] we regard the negligence standard of fault applicable to public nuisance as likely to be no more than an antiquated relic of its history as a tortious form of wrongdoing. In that regard, in our report on offences against the person[24] we said:

> Actions that may be thought culpable, because negligent, in terms of the law of civil liability are not necessarily enough to attract criminal liability: because principles of personal autonomy and freedom require that the state should only use its machinery to inflict punishment on those who know what they are doing, and thus could, but do not choose to, desist.

5.23 Further, these comparable offences are most emphatically not ones of strict or no-fault liability.

5.24 Some of the analogous offences involve an element of so-called 'constructive' liability, even though they employ intention and recklessness (or its equivalent) as fault elements. That is to say, such offences involve a requirement for proof of fault only as to the (independently criminal) conduct element and *not* as to the consequence element. Liability respecting the consequence element is accordingly, if somewhat misleadingly, called 'constructive'.[25]

5.25 An example is assault occasioning actual bodily harm, contrary to section 47 of the Offences Against the Person Act 1861. Someone can be convicted of this offence when they have 'occasioned' actual bodily harm through an assault, if they are shown to have intended an assault, or been reckless concerning whether an assault might result from their conduct. It is not relevant to liability

---

[23] Paras 5.34 to 5.41.

[24] Legislating the Criminal Code: Offences against the Person and General Principles (1993) Law Com No 218 para 14.14.

[25] For a sophisticated examination of the 'constructive' element in criminal liability, see AP Simester, "Is Strict Liability Always Wrong?"; John Spencer and Antje Pedain, "Approaches to Strict and Constructive Liability in Continental Criminal Law", both in AP Simester (ed.) *Appraising Strict Liability* (2005).

whether or not they intended or realised that they might cause actual bodily harm (the 'constructive' element of the offence).[26]

5.26 Whether or not an element of constructive liability is justified when it occurs in the offences mentioned above is not an issue that need concern us here.[27] This is because we are provisionally proposing that, in both public nuisance and outraging public decency, D must be proved either to have intended the conduct and consequence elements to occur, or to have realised that they might occur, as a result of his or her conduct. Does this formulation avoid any element of strict or constructive liability? It will do so, if understood in the following way.

5.27 If the fault element (intention or recklessness) is proven, it should not be relevant that D did not personally believe that his or her conduct should be regarded as a public nuisance, or as outraging public decency. That would open up an unjustified gap in the law's coverage. Adopting this approach might however give rise to a situation in which, whilst intending the physical acts at issue, D was – perhaps quite understandably – wholly unaware of possibility that the acts might in fact be regarded as a public nuisance or as an outrage to public decency. If liability could established in such a case, it would involve a kind of strict liability, liability without fault.[28]

5.28 Accordingly, our provisional proposal must be understood as subject to the following rider. A 'public nuisance' or an instance of 'outraging public decency' is involved when the conduct in question is what ordinary people would regard as a public nuisance or as an outrage to public decency. The fault element will be proven only if D is shown to have intended to cause such a nuisance or outrage, or to have realised that such a nuisance or outrage – one regarded by ordinary people as such – might be caused by his or her conduct.

5.29 Given that it will be sufficient to show that D realised that his or her conduct might cause a nuisance, or might outrage public decency in the eyes of the ordinary person, our proposal is analogous to the approach taken in law to offences where a question arises concerning whether or not conduct was 'dishonest'. The key issue in cases where dishonesty is an element of the crime is not whether D personally believed his or her conduct to be dishonest. The key issue is whether D realised that reasonable and honest people would regard that conduct as dishonest.[29]

5.30 Almost all of the analogous offences mentioned are imprisonable offences. This is, of course, a feature that they share with both public nuisance and outraging public decency. Any offence commission of which may be met a sentence of imprisonment should be regarded as truly criminal in nature, and not a merely administrative or regulatory transgression.

[26] *Savage; Parmenter* [1992] 1 AC 699.

[27] As we saw in Part 2, in some jurisdictions where nuisance has been codified, there is a similar form of constructive liability. For example, under s 180 of the Canadian Criminal Code, D will be guilty of common nuisance when, amongst other instances, he or she "commits a common nuisance" (the conduct element) which, "causes physical injury to any person" (the consequence element, 'constructively' attributed to D irrespective of fault).

[28] See the discussion in *Smith and Hogan* at para 7.1 (pp 150-53).

[29] See *Ghosh* [1982] QB 1053.

5.31 That does not imply that negligence, or other kinds of inadvertent fault, cannot be sufficient to justify a sentence of imprisonment when some kinds of harm are done, or risks posed, in consequence. The examples given earlier of rape, and of dangerous driving, together with gross negligence at common law, show that this implication should not be drawn. However, there must be an adequate, context-based justification for creating an imprisonable offence, respecting harm done or risk posed merely through negligence (or its equivalent).

PUBLIC NUISANCE

5.32 As we have seen,[30] the existing test of fault in public nuisance is essentially an objective, negligence-based one. Andrew Ashworth, in the case note cited above,[31] drew attention to one point certified by the Court of Appeal in *Rimmington* as being of public importance, namely:

> whether it is sufficient to prove that the defendant ought to have known of the risk that public nuisance would be caused by his behaviour, or whether (after *G*[32]) proof of awareness of the risk should be required.

Counsel for Goldstein submitted that *Shorrock* was wrongly decided and that the *G* test, of recklessness should be applied. The House of Lords did not give any detailed consideration to this proposal, but simply asserted that the *Shorrock* test was correct in light of previous authority and that *G* turned on a statutory definition in which the word "reckless" was specifically mentioned.[33] As they proceeded to hold that Goldstein was not guilty even on the *Shorrock* test there was no need for a critical examination of this assumption. From the point of view of law reform one may regard this as a missed opportunity.

5.33 It might be asked why the courts never applied a subjective test of fault, such as whether there had been 'malice' in causing the nuisance, in much the same way that malice was employed, for example, in the law of homicide and in the Acts of 1861 governing some non-fatal offences and criminal damage.[34] The answer probably lies in the peculiar position that nuisance occupies on the borderline between tort and crime.

5.34 The primary remedy in tort cases has always been a civil action by individuals, commonly involving proof of negligence on the part of the tortfeasor. However, where the injured party was not a neighbouring individual occupier but the public, the wrong had to be framed as an offence, because by definition there was no such thing as civil proceedings brought by the public. Had the law always employed a category of administrative enforcement proceedings of a modern type, public nuisance would have been put in this category. This is shown by the facts that, at one period, the main use of public nuisance was as a springboard

---

[30] Para 2.36 and following.

[31] Para 4.13.

[32] [2003] UKHL 50, [2004] 1 AC 1034.

[33] *Rimmington* paras 39, 56.

[34] Respectively, the Offences Against the Person Act 1861 and the Malicious Damage Act 1861 (now replaced by the Criminal Damage Act 1971).

allowing the Attorney General to bring proceedings for an injunction[35] and that, when a prosecution does take place, the court on conviction may order the removal of the nuisance.[36]

5.35 This was quite frankly confessed by Mellor J in *Stephens*,[37] who said:

> the only reason for proceeding criminally is that the nuisance, instead of being merely a nuisance affecting an individual, or one or two individuals, affects the public at large, and no private individual, without receiving some special injury, could have maintained an action. Then if the contention of those who say the direction is wrong is to prevail, the public would have great difficulty in getting redress.

In other words, criminal proceedings were only allowed because there was no other remedy. In modern conditions, with the wealth of statutory environmental offences and remedies, none of which require proof of a guilty state of mind, this argument no longer holds water and there is no excuse for using criminal prosecutions as a substitute for an action in tort or a public law regulatory remedy.

5.36 The tort test may not always have applied to all instances of the offence. Following *Stephens* it remained arguable that the tort-like character of nuisance, with its consequences of an objective test of fault and vicarious liability, only held for the "core" nuisances with a clear analogy to private nuisance, and that the remaining instances, being essentially public order offences, should be treated as genuinely criminal.[38] However, *Shorrock*[39] appeared to suggest that the objective test was the general one, and *Rimmington*, by retrenching the offence more closely around the "core" nuisances, could be taken as indirectly confirming this tendency.

5.37 This appears to us to be inconsistent with the use of the offence in practice. As we have seen,[40] most prosecutions for the common law offence fall within the behavioural category, and even within the environmental category that offence is properly reserved for the more flagrant examples of wilful conduct.[41]

5.38 Under the modern law, many offences that might previously have had to be prosecuted as nuisance cases can now be prosecuted as one of a large number of largely regulatory offences concerned with environmental protection.[42] This means that nuisance is likely to be charged not only where a 'gap' that it can fill between such offences has appeared, but also more importantly where the nature of D's conduct is such as to warrant charging a more serious, common law

---

[35] Spencer, pp 70-71.

[36] Bl Comm iv 167-8; *Archbold* para 31-49; *Incledon* (1810) 13 East 164, 104 ER 331.

[37] Para 2.43 above.

[38] For this distinction see para 2.11 above.

[39] Para 2.38 and following, above.

[40] Paras 2.46 to 2.51.

[41] Para 4.19.

[42] Para 2.53 and following.

offence. Examples might be where D brings a personal dispute with a local authority to public attention by spreading a foul-smelling and potentially harmful liquid on the pavement outside the Town Hall, or where D persistently engages in hoaxes that lead gullible members of the public unwittingly to engage in dangerous or demeaning conduct.

5.39 As we said at the outset, we are not challenging the applicability or usefulness of the crime of nuisance in such cases. However, what we do believe is that it is no longer appropriate that nuisance retains its negligence-based fault element. That is an echo of its life as a kind of 'public tort', or as an old-fashioned catch-all substitute for regulatory offences (many of which employ such 'objective' fault elements).

5.40 We are not convinced that there is any need for absolute identity between the requirements for the tort and the crime of public nuisance because of the identity of name. The offence of assault, for example, is equally closely associated with the tort of trespass to the person, but the courts have experienced no difficulty in holding that criminal assault requires full intention or recklessness while negligence is sufficient for trespass to the person.[43] Another dual-character wrong is false imprisonment, where the tort is one of strict liability[44] while the crime must be "intentional or reckless".[45]

5.41 We have no intention of altering the existence or ingredients of the tort or the basis on which the Attorney-General and local authorities can apply for an injunction to stop a nuisance. Nor do we believe that altering, or even abolishing, the offence would have this effect.[46] The reasoning in cases in which injunctions are sought always appears to be based on public nuisance as a tort rather than as a crime.[47] In *Zain*,[48] it had to be clarified that a local authority had power to restrain a nuisance *although* it also amounted to a crime and local authorities have no general duty of suppressing criminality. In other words, the tort is fundamental: the availability of criminal proceedings and the availability of injunctions are two parallel outgrowths from it, neither of which depends on the other. The requirement of damage peculiar to an individual in tort cases is a purely pragmatic restraint designed to avoid multiplicity of actions, and affects only an individual's right to sue for damages, and not the existence of the tort as such.

5.42 As explained in Part 2[49] instances of public nuisance can be divided broadly into environmental and behavioural categories. The environmental cases may be

---

[43] A claim for negligent injury that is direct and forcible can be framed in trespass, though the limitation provisions are the same as those for negligence: *Letang v Cooper* [1965] 1 QB 232. See *Clerk and Lindsell on Torts* para 1.46.

[44] *R v Governor of Brockhill Prison ex parte Evans* [1997] QB 443.

[45] *Rahman* (1985) 81 Cr App R 349, 353.

[46] In this we differ from Spencer, p 80, who says that "if the crime of public nuisance were completely abolished, with it would also go the possibility of obtaining an injunction to stop one".

[47] *Attorney General v PYA Quarries Ltd* [1957] 2 QB 169, *Nottingham City Council v Zain* [2001] EWCA Civ 1248, [2002] 1 WLR 607.

[48] [2001] EWCA Civ 1248, [2002] 1 WLR 607.

suitable for a regulatory approach; if so they are likely to be already covered by regulatory law such as that created by the Environmental Protection Act 1990 and by local authority bye-laws. Both in local authority and in police practice, the common law offence is generally reserved for the more serious instances of misbehaviour, with or without an environmental effect.

5.43 Given that public nuisance is so reserved, in practice, we believe that it should have the same fault elements as imprisonable offences that tend to cover similar ground, at broadly the same level of gravity.

5.44 We provisionally propose that public nuisance should be found proved only when D is shown to have acted in the relevant respect intentionally or recklessly with regard to the creation of a public nuisance. That is, D must be shown to have intended to create, or realised that he or she might generate, what ordinary people would regard as a public nuisance.

OUTRAGING PUBLIC DECENCY

5.45 Turning to the crime of outraging public decency, this currently involves a very significant element of strict liability. So long as D intended the relevant conduct to take place, it is quite irrelevant not only whether D personally thought the conduct indecent, but also whether he or she realised that it might be regarded as indecent by others, or even that it might be seen at all.[50] D is treated as if he or she intended to outrage public decency or was aware that this might happen simply because he or she intended to do the act that had this effect (even though that act is not in itself need not be criminal). This kind of strict liability is arguably more objectionable than the merely constructive liability found in, say, the offence of assault occasioning actual bodily harm, discussed above.[51] In the latter case, D must at least be shown to have had the fault element for, and hence have committed, a conduct crime – assault – before it becomes appropriate to fix him or her with (constructive) liability for the consequences – occasioning actual bodily harm. There is no such 'threshold' requirement for criminal activity before liability is imposed in cases of outraging public decency.

5.46 A conviction for outraging public decency carries considerable stigma. It is also, of course, an imprisonable offence. Bearing in mind that it will may well share a good deal in common with the other imprisonable offences that we mentioned earlier – such as some public order offences, criminal damage, and some offences against the person – we believe that it should be reformed so that it shares a similar approach, in terms of fault.

5.47 As with public nuisance we consider that, as the offence carries a considerable stigma as well as a power of imprisonment, it is unacceptable that it can be committed inadvertently. This is especially so in those public decency cases where the defendant had no reason to believe that his or her activities would be observed at all.

---

[49] Para 2.46.

[50] Paras 3.39 to 3.42 above.

[51] Para 5.25.

5.48   It might be objected that, if the law were changed in such cases, defendants on facts such as *Hamilton* would escape liability: as mentioned above, he was clearly counting on not being seen. In such cases, however, a jury would most probably conclude that the defendant must have realised that he might be detected by one of the intended victims, and that if he was detected this was bound to cause quite reasonable offence.

5.49   The cases where the disagreement is about the standard of indecency are more finely balanced. Arguments for preserving the existing law are as follows.

   (1)   As in the case of rape, it is not unreasonable to insist that a person proposing to do something which could be very offensive and intrusive if not agreed to should have the onus of making quite sure that it is agreed to: in this case, that there is nothing that the public will find offensive.

   (2)   As argued in *Gibson and Sylveire*,[52] to make the defendant's own opinions on indecency the standard is to make him the judge in his own cause.

5.50   The answer to both arguments is that the proposed criterion is not the defendant's private view of indecency but the assessment of the chance that two or more members of the public will in fact be disgusted, whether reasonably (in the defendant's view) or not. In many cases the offensive nature of the display will be obvious; and while, since the Criminal Justice Act 1967, there is no longer a presumption that a person intends the natural and probable consequences of his acts, it will still be the case that, in the words of Lord Lane CJ:[53]

> Although that presumption which I have just mentioned no longer of course exists, nevertheless, where one has a display of, such as, foetus earrings in the instant case, once the outrage is established to the satisfaction of the jury, the defendant is scarcely likely to be believed if he says that he was not aware of the danger he was running of causing offence and outrage to the public. Indeed had the judge in the present case directed the jury along the lines it is suggested he should have directed them,[54] there can be no doubt, in our minds, that in the case of each appellant the result would have been the same, and a conviction would have been recorded.

It is only in these cases of obvious offensiveness that argument (1) (the rape analogy) holds, so that the defendant must be taken as knowing that the activities are potentially outrageous and must therefore take full responsibility for the risk of disgusting the public.

5.51   A final point is that the test of recklessness means, not only that the defendant was aware of the risk, but also that despite that knowledge he or she unjustifiably decided to proceed. This may provide an answer to the claim that the offence of outraging public decency, even as modified by our proposals, imports an excessive degree of artistic censorship. Where the work is truly of artistic

---

[52]   Para 3.42 above.

[53]   *Gibson and Sylveire* [1990] 2 QB 619, 629.

[54]   Namely a recklessness test.

importance, the jury can always find that, though the effect of outraging the public was foreseeable and indeed foreseen, the decision to take the risk was justified.

5.52 **We provisionally propose that outraging public decency should be found proved only when D is shown to have acted in the relevant respect intentionally or recklessly with regard to the outraging of public decency. That is, D must be shown to have intended to generate, or realised that he or she might generate, outrage, shock or disgust in ordinary people.**

PART 6
RESTATING THE OFFENCES IN STATUTE

PUBLIC NUISANCE

6.1 We consider that the arguments set out above show that there is no clear case for either abolishing the offence or significantly restricting or altering its conduct element, but that the fault element should be revised to require at least recklessness. The question arises whether this should be done by a simple statutory provision to that effect or whether we should use this opportunity to put the whole definition of the offence into statutory form.

6.2 We are strongly of the view that defining the offence by statute is desirable in principle. Restating the offence in statutory form will aid any ultimate codification of criminal law, an important part of the Law Commission's long-term aims.[1] Taking such a step would also remove or avoid any doubt about the constitutional legitimacy or human rights desirability of perpetuating the results of judicial law-making.[2] Not to codify the offence now is to leave the same question for a later project in which full codification is envisaged.

6.3 The argument against codification is that there are technical difficulties in restating the existing law in statutory form and that any such restatement might reduce the breadth and flexibility of the offence, which prosecutors find convenient. One answer to that is that, if the flexibility of the offence were so great as to make codification technically impossible, that very fact would show that the existing offence falls foul of the constitutional and human rights requirements of legal certainty. As argued above,[3] flexibility beyond a certain point becomes an undesirable luxury.

6.4 The next question is whether to follow the textbook definition of the offence, for example the form found in *Archbold*, or to try to find an alternative.

6.5 The argument for using the textbook definition is that it has been accepted by the House of Lords in *Rimmington* as an authoritative statement of the law, and that similar definitions have been used with no adverse consequences in other Commonwealth countries.[4] While the present project does not form part of a programme of full codification, the simplicity of the definition makes placing this particular offence in statutory form an easily achieved aim in a programme of simplification.

6.6 The argument against using the textbook definition is that it would not increase the certainty of the offence. The debates in *Rimmington* would have been little if at all shorter had a definition in that form already been enacted. Further, the formula "act not warranted by law or omission to perform a public duty" is

---

[1] Law Commissions Act 1965 s 3(1).

[2] Paras 4.8 to 4.10.

[3] Para 4.7.

[4] Except possibly Canada: see the discussion of *Thornton* in paras 2.67 and 6.6(1).

problematic.[5] There is force in Spencer's argument that this formula is suitable only as a generic description of a category of offences, or even of a power of creating offences, and not of an actual offence.[6] It is not clear whether the law and duty in question refer to identifiable legal duties that do not themselves depend on the law of nuisance, and the definition could be circular. Were the *Archbold* definition enacted in statutory form, one of two things would happen.

(1) The whole definition could be taken seriously, and every case would require detailed investigation of whether the act was truly unlawful or what duty had been omitted, as in the Canadian case of *Thornton*.[7] This would complicate the law rather than simplifying it.

(2) Alternatively, the first part of the definition could be taken as a rhetorical generality, serving only as a hook for the requirement of public injury and an acknowledgment of a defence of specific statutory justification. This would in effect leave the question of whether a nuisance exists to be resolved as it was at common law, and codification would perform no function (but also do no harm).

6.7 We consider on balance that it would be preferable to explore alternative definitions. The purpose of any such definition would be to preserve the requirement of common injury while keeping the scope of the act or omission causing that injury as wide as possible.

Provisional proposal

6.8 **We provisionally propose:**

(1) **to restate the offence in statutory form, while altering the fault element as proposed above;[8]**

(2) **for this purpose, to explore definitions alternative to that given in *Archbold*.**

6.9 **Consultees are asked for their views on how the offence of public nuisance should best be defined by statute to give effect to the above proposal.**

Sentencing

6.10 If the offence of public nuisance is restated in statutory form, it may be desirable to consider at the same time whether to alter the sentencing powers, for example by providing for a fixed maximum sentence. This is a matter to be considered by the Government department sponsoring any legislation resulting from our proposals.

6.11 We envisage that the offence of public nuisance, with the strengthened fault element as proposed, will be used mainly for instances of wilful and serious

---

[5] Para 2.9 above.

[6] Para 2.10 above.

[7] Para 2.67 above.

[8] At para 5.44.

misbehaviour for which the existing specialised statutory offences are not adequate. Any fixed maximum sentence provided by statute should therefore be considerably in excess of that for the specialised offences.

OUTRAGING PUBLIC DECENCY

6.12 As with public nuisance, the question arises whether the opportunity should be taken to restate the offence in statutory form; and for the reasons given above[9] we are strongly of the opinion that this is desirable.

6.13 Some work will need to be done to produce a workable statutory definition. Provisionally, an outline definition might look something like the following.

    (1)   The conduct element would be performing any activity or creating any display or object:

        (a)   which is of such a nature as to be likely to cause a reasonable person witnessing it shock, outrage or humiliation (the indecency requirement),

        (b)   in such a place or in such circumstances that it may be witnessed by two or more members of the public (the publicity requirement).

    (2)   The fault element would be intention that these two conditions (indecency and publicity) obtain, or recklessness as to whether they will obtain.

6.14 The effect of this will not be, as such, to simplify the particular offence (except insofar as any codification simplifies access to the law). Its effect will be to simplify the overall criminal law governing several analogous offences, by reducing the number of unnecessary distinctions.

Provisional proposals

6.15 We provisionally propose:

    (1)   to restate the offence in statutory form, while altering the fault element as proposed above;[10]

    (2)   for this purpose, to use a definition on the lines suggested in paragraph 6.13 above;

    (3)   to amend the Criminal Law Act 1977 so as to abolish the common law offence of conspiracy to outrage public decency.

---

[9]   Paras 6.2 and 6.3.

[10]   Para 5.52.

Sentencing

6.16 As with public nuisance,[11] any statutory restatement of the offence of outraging public decency should be accompanied by a reconsideration of the appropriate powers of sentencing.

---

[11] Para 6.10.

PART 7
PROVISIONAL PROPOSALS AND QUESTIONS FOR CONSULTATION

Public nuisance

7.1 We provisionally propose that the offence of public nuisance be retained, and that its conduct element should remain in its present form as laid down in *Rimmington*. (Paragraph 4.27)

7.2 We provisionally propose that public nuisance should be found proved only when D is shown to have acted in the relevant respect intentionally or recklessly with regard to the creation of a public nuisance. That is, D must be shown to have intended to create, or realised that he or she might generate, what ordinary people would regard as a public nuisance. (Paragraph 5.44)

7.3 We provisionally propose:

(1) to restate the offence in statutory form, while altering the fault element as proposed above;[1]

(2) for this purpose, to explore definitions alternative to that given in *Archbold*.

7.4 Consultees are asked for their views on how the offence of public nuisance should best be defined by statute to give effect to the above proposal. (Paragraphs 6.8 and 6.9)

Outraging public decency

7.5 We provisionally propose that the offence of outraging public decency be retained, and that its conduct element should remain in its present form as laid down in *Hamilton*. (Paragraph 4.43)

7.6 We provisionally propose that outraging public decency should be found proved only when D is shown to have acted in the relevant respect intentionally or recklessly with regard to the outraging of public decency. That is, D must be shown to have intended to generate, or realised that he or she might generate, outrage, shock or disgust in ordinary people. (Paragraph 5.52)

7.7 We provisionally propose:

(1) to restate the offence in statutory form, while altering the fault element as proposed above;[2]

(2) for this purpose, to use a definition on the lines suggested in paragraph 6.13 above;

---

[1] At para 7.2.

[2] Para 7.6.

(3)   to amend the Criminal Law Act 1977 so as to abolish the common law offence of conspiracy to outrage public decency. (Paragraph 6.15)

Additional questions for consultation

7.8   Consultees are asked for any further information they can contribute on the existing practice relating to the offences of public nuisance and outraging public decency and to the alternative offences, remedies and procedures as described in this paper.

7.9   An impact assessment accompanies this paper. Consultees are asked if they have any comments to make on this assessment, or more generally on the likely impact of the proposed changes.

APPENDIX A
IMPACT ASSESSMENT FOR REFORMING THE OFFENCES OF PUBLIC NUISANCE AND OUTRAGING PUBLIC DECENCY

Summary: Intervention & Options

Department /Agency: Law Commission	Title: Impact Assessment of draft CP on public nuisance	
Stage: Consultation Paper	Version:	Date: March 2010

Related Publications: Simplification of Criminal Law: Public Nuisance and Outraging Public Decency (Consultation Paper)

Available to view or download at:

http://www.lawcom.gov.uk/docs/cp193.pdf

Contact for enquiries: criminal@lawcommission.gsi.gov.uk   **Telephone:** 020 3334 0200

What is the problem under consideration? Why is government intervention necessary?

The offences of public nuisance and outraging public decency have been criticised for being vague and for covering too wide a spectrum of behaviour, and some have argued that they are unnecessary. The scope of the offences has been narrowed and made more certain by the recent cases of *Rimmington* (for public nuisance) and *Hamilton* (for outraging public decency). However it remains possible to commit both offences inadvertently and without intentional or reckless conduct. This is inconsistent with the position for most offences of comparable facts and gravity.

Government intervention is necessary because the position can only be changed by statute.

What are the policy objectives and the intended effects?

The policy objective is to make the law relating to both offences clearer and fairer, and to ensure that the sanction is more in keeping with the gravity and character of the conduct addressed.

The intended effect is that only intentional or reckless conduct will incur liability for these offences. This will mean that a person is not exposed to the risk of imprisonment for merely negligent or inadvertent instances of the behaviour in question.

What policy options have been considered? Please justify any preferred option.

Option 1: do nothing.

Option 2: enact a statute providing that, to be guilty of either public nuisance or outraging public decency, the defendant must either have intended the adverse effects of his or her conduct ("intention"), or been aware of the risk of those effects and nevertheless decided, without reasonable justification, to engage in that conduct ("recklessness").

Option 3: enact a statute abolishing the common law offences of public nuisance and outraging public decency and creating statutory offences in their place, with an intention or recklessness standard.

Option 4: abolish both offences without replacement. For reasons shown below, we prefer 3.

When will the policy be reviewed to establish the actual costs and benefits and the achievement of the desired effects?

Ministerial Sign-off For final proposal/implementation stage Impact Assessments:

I have read the Impact Assessment and I am satisfied that (a) it represents a fair and reasonable view of the expected costs, benefits and impact of the policy, and (b) the benefits justify the costs.

Signed by the responsible Minister:

....Date:

Summary: Analysis & Evidence

Policy Option: 2	Description: Amend existing statutory provisions

COSTS

ANNUAL COSTS	Description and scale of **key monetised costs** by 'main affected groups'
One-off (Transition) **Yrs**	The reduction in prosecutions (below) may lead to a small increase in the use of alternative procedures, such as specialised offences and enforcement notices, and in civil actions.
£ **Negligible**	
Average Annual Cost (excluding one-off)	
£ **Negligible**	**Total Cost** (PV) £ **Negligible**

Other **key non-monetised costs** by 'main affected groups'

BENEFITS

ANNUAL BENEFITS	Description and scale of key monetised benefits by 'main affected groups'
One-off **Yrs**	There should be a reduction in prosecutions, with some saving in costs. Clearer, more consistent law will be less likely to be subject to legal challenge thereby resulting in savings in court, prosecution and defence costs.
£	
Average Annual Benefit (excluding one-off)	
£	**Total Benefit** (PV) £

Other **key non-monetised benefits** by 'main affected groups'

This option would ensure that defendants are only convicted of public nuisance and outraging public decency (both serious imprisonable offences) for deliberate conduct in full consciousness of the risks. This should increase public perception that the law is fair.

Key Assumptions/Sensitivities/Risks

Key assumption: local authorities, the police and the CPS already only use public nuisance where other procedures are unsuitable. Narrowing the offences should lead to little if any increase in the use of other procedures. Risk: more issues may arise where intention is unclear.

Price Base Year	Time Period Years	Net Benefit Range (NPV) £	NET BENEFIT (NPV Best estimate) £

What is the geographic coverage of the policy/option?	England and Wales
On what date will the policy be implemented?	
Which organisation(s) will enforce the policy?	Courts, prosecutors
What is the total annual cost of enforcement for these organisations?	£ Negligible
Does enforcement comply with Hampton principles?	Not applicable
Will implementation go beyond minimum EU requirements?	Not applicable
What is the value of the proposed offsetting measure per year?	£ Not applicable
What is the value of changes in greenhouse gas emissions?	£ Not applicable
Will the proposal have a significant impact on competition?	No

Annual cost (£-£) per organisation (excluding one-off)	Micro	Small	Medium	Large
Are any of these organisations exempt?	Yes/No	Yes/No	N/A	N/A

Impact on Admin Burdens Baseline (2005 Prices)		(Increase - Decrease)
Increase of £ Decrease of £	**Net Impact**	£ None anticipated

Key: Annual costs and benefits: Constant Prices   (Net) Present Value

Summary: Analysis & Evidence

Policy Option: 3	Description: Abolish the existing offences and create new statutory offences

COSTS

ANNUAL COSTS			Description and scale of key monetised costs by 'main affected groups'
One-off (Transition)		**Yrs**	The creation of new offences might generate initial uncertainty and some increased litigation while the boundaries are tested. Otherwise, effects are the same as for option 2.
£ Small		1-2	
Average Annual Cost (excluding one-off)			
£ Negligible			**Total Cost** (PV) £

Other **key non-monetised costs** by 'main affected groups'

The main suggestion so far for a statutory formula ("act not warranted by law or omission to discharge a legal duty") might complicate the law rather than simplifying it. We propose to work on devising an alternative formula that would avoid this problem.

BENEFITS

ANNUAL BENEFITS			Description and scale of **key monetised benefits** by 'main affected groups'
One-off		**Yrs**	As for option 2
£			
Average Annual Benefit (excluding one-off)			
£			**Total Benefit** (PV) £

Other **key non-monetised benefits** by 'main affected groups'

As for option 2. Also, full codification leads to greater legal certainty in the long run and saves the need for further work if it is later decided to codify the criminal law as a whole.

Key Assumptions/Sensitivities/Risks

Key assumption: that we shall be able to devise a statutory formula which accurately represents the current law, as modified by our proposals on fault. Risk: that the definition of the act or omission causing the common injury would create an extra hurdle.

Price Base Year	Time Period Years	Net Benefit Range (NPV) £	NET BENEFIT (NPV Best estimate) £

What is the geographic coverage of the policy/option?	England and Wales
On what date will the policy be implemented?	
Which organisation(s) will enforce the policy?	Courts, prosecutors
What is the total annual cost of enforcement for these organisations?	£ Negligible
Does enforcement comply with Hampton principles?	Not applicable
Will implementation go beyond minimum EU requirements?	Not applicable
What is the value of the proposed offsetting measure per year?	£ Not applicable
What is the value of changes in greenhouse gas emissions?	£ Not applicable
Will the proposal have a significant impact on competition?	No

Annual cost (£-£) per organisation (excluding one-off)	Micro	Small	Medium	Large
Are any of these organisations exempt?	Yes/No	Yes/No	N/A	N/A

Impact on Admin Burdens Baseline (2005 Prices)		(Increase - Decrease)	
Increase of £	Decrease of £	**Net Impact**	£ None anticipated

Summary: Analysis & Evidence

Policy Option: 4	Description: Abolish the existing offences without replacement

COSTS

ANNUAL COSTS	Description and scale of **key monetised costs** by 'main affected groups'
One-off (Transition) **Yrs**	The abolition of these offences might lead to an increase in the use of other procedures.
£ Negligible	
Average Annual Cost (excluding one-off)	
£	**Total Cost** (PV) £

Other **key non-monetised costs** by 'main affected groups'

Prosecutors would be limited to using narrow and specialised offences and procedures, which do not adequately reflect the scope or the gravity of the more serious and flagrant instances of misbehaviour, and may not keep up with innovations in anti-social behaviour.

BENEFITS

ANNUAL BENEFITS	Description and scale of **key monetised benefits** by 'main affected groups'
One-off **Yrs**	There would be a saving of the cost of anything up to a thousand prosecutions in each year, partially offset by the use of other procedures.
£	
Average Annual Benefit (excluding one-off)	
£	**Total Benefit** (PV) £

Other **key non-monetised benefits** by 'main affected groups'

Defendants would not be prosecuted for offences of uncertain scope which target negligent or inadvertent behaviour (this benefit is common to options 2, 3 and 4)

Key Assumptions/Sensitivities/Risks

Key assumption: statistics provided by the CPS and local authorities are correct and representative. Risk: that some perpetrators of wilful or persistent misbehaviour would remain unprosecuted, or be prosecuted for minor offences that do not reflect the seriousness of what occurred.

Price Base Year	Time Period Years	Net Benefit Range (NPV) £	NET BENEFIT (NPV Best estimate) £

What is the geographic coverage of the policy/option?	England and Wales
On what date will the policy be implemented?	
Which organisation(s) will enforce the policy?	Courts, prosecutors
What is the total annual cost of enforcement for these organisations?	£ Negligible
Does enforcement comply with Hampton principles?	Not applicable
Will implementation go beyond minimum EU requirements?	Not applicable
What is the value of the proposed offsetting measure per year?	£ Not applicable
What is the value of changes in greenhouse gas emissions?	£ Not applicable
Will the proposal have a significant impact on competition?	No

Annual cost (£-£) per organisation (excluding one-off)	Micro	Small	Medium	Large
Are any of these organisations exempt?	Yes/No	Yes/No	N/A	N/A

Impact on Admin Burdens Baseline (2005 Prices)		(Increase - Decrease)
Increase of £	Decrease of £	**Net Impact** £ None anticipated

Evidence Base (for summary sheets)

[Use this space (with a recommended maximum of 30 pages) to set out the evidence, analysis and detailed narrative from which you have generated your policy options or proposal. Ensure that the information is organised in such a way as to explain clearly the summary information on the preceding pages of this form.]

PROBLEMS UNDER CONSIDERATION

Existing law

Public nuisance

Very broadly, public nuisance is any unwarranted conduct that affects the safety or comfort of the public, either in general or in a given area. One established definition is:

> A person is guilty of a public nuisance (also known as common nuisance), who (a) does an act not warranted by law, or (b) omits to discharge a legal duty, if the effect of the act or omission is to endanger the life, health, property or comfort of the public, or to obstruct the public in the exercise or enjoyment of rights common to all Her Majesty's subjects.

It can be divided roughly between environmental nuisances (pollution, noise, obstructions) and behavioural nuisances (offensive behaviour in public). In some cases, especially those concerning noise, the two will overlap.

Examples of public nuisance are:

(1)   obstructing the highway;

(2)   blasting and quarrying near built-up areas;

(3)   allowing land to be used as a dump, creating a dangerous or noxious environment;

(4)   noisy parties and "raves";

(5)   bomb hoaxes and false calls to the emergency services;

(6)   hanging from motorways and bridges, for example in political demonstrations;

(7)   keeping pumas in a domestic garden;

(8)   gang activity involving drug dealing in an urban area.[1]

Public nuisance can be used in three ways. First, as a criminal offence: it is only this aspect with which we are concerned in this project. Secondly, an individual particularly affected by a public nuisance can sue in tort. Thirdly, the Attorney General, the local authority or the person affected can apply for an injunction.

---

[1]   The significance of this last example is not that those responsible are prosecuted for public nuisance (there are more appropriate offences) but that injunctions can be granted.

The outlines of the offence were clarified in the recent case of *Rimmington*.[2] This confirmed that a public nuisance must affect the public collectively. A series of acts against individuals, such as hate mail or obscene telephone calls, does not qualify.

The required state of mind for the criminal offence is negligence: the defendant ought reasonably to have foreseen the adverse consequences of his or her conduct. This was confirmed in Goldstein, an appeal heard together with *Rimmington*.

Outraging public decency

Outraging public decency means performing indecent activities or setting up an indecent display in such a place and way that more than one member of the public may see and be offended by it. It can include publications, provided that these are liable to shock and disgust, as opposed to being liable to corrupt and deprave, in which case the offence under the Obscene Publications Acts must be used.

The required state of mind for outraging public decency is mixed. The defendant must have intended to perform the activity or set up the display. The defendant need not have known or intended it to be indecent, in the sense of likely to offend if seen: if it is in fact indecent that is sufficient. For that matter, the defendant need not have known that it might be seen at all.

The outlines of the offence were clarified in *Rose v DPP*[3] (concerning a sexual act performed in view of a bank's CCTV equipment) and *Hamilton*[4] (concerning a person filming up women's skirts). The essence of the offence is the risk of public offence: namely that, whether or not anyone actually saw it, the circumstances were such that two or more people could have seen and been offended.

Reasons for reform

Public nuisance and outraging public decency are both serious offences carrying a potential prison sentence, but it is possible to incur liability for both through inadvertent or negligent behaviour. This is a different standard of blame from that applying to most offences with similar facts and of comparable gravity.

Criminal damage, for example, requires the defendant to be "intending to destroy or damage any such property or being reckless as to whether any such property would be destroyed or damaged". This would be the appropriate standard to apply to public nuisance.

In the offence of outraging public decency, at present there is no requirement that the defendant should have known or believed that the spectacle was indecent, in the sense of being likely to offend the public. However, indecency in this sense is the essence of the offence. The appropriate standard of blame is that the defendant either intended to cause public outrage or was reckless as to whether outrage would be caused.

---

[2]   [2006] 1 AC 459 (HL).

[3]   [2006] 1 WLR 2626.

[4]   [2008] QB 224.

RATIONALE FOR GOVERNMENT INTERVENTION

It is in the public interest that the law of public nuisance and outraging public decency should be perceived to be fair. Recent cases have established the standard of blame for both offences: in the case of public nuisance the relevant case was decided by the House of Lords. Any reform must therefore be effected by legislation.

POLICY OBJECTIVES

1. To make the law relating to both offences fit the gravity of the kind of conduct addressed, and ensure that the standard of blame is similar to that of comparable offences.

2. To ensure that blameworthy conduct falls within the scope of these offences and that non-blameworthy conduct falls outside it.

3. To clarify the existing law and provide for greater legal certainty.

SCALE AND CONTEXT

Public nuisance

At present approximately 250 prosecutions for this offence are brought every year by the Crown Prosecution Service. An unknown further number are brought by local authorities: on anecdotal evidence, we believe that these amount to fewer than one a year per authority, so that the total number is smaller than in the case of the CPS.

The CPS prosecutions generally relate to wilful and flagrant examples of misbehaviour in public. As our proposal is to exempt from liability only those nuisances that are merely negligent, it should not have a significant effect on these prosecutions.

Environmental nuisances are generally dealt with by local authorities. However, they prefer to deal with them by using statutory powers, for example under the Environmental Protection Act 1990 and under bye-laws. Prosecution is an option of last resort, and prosecution for public nuisance, as opposed to prosecution under statutory powers, is still rarer. It is generally reserved for the most serious and persistent instances of nuisance. As with the CPS prosecutions, our proposal should simply confirm existing practice.

A further category of public nuisance is wilful or negligent acts that have the effect of obstructing public access or disrupting public services. An example would be the case of *Goldstein*, where a person enclosed a small quantity of salt in an envelope as a joke, and this leaked in the sorting office and caused an anthrax scare. On the facts, this was found to be not even negligent, and the defendant was not liable. One could however imagine similar facts in which the defendant's conduct was negligent but not wilful or reckless, as alleged by the prosecution in *Goldstein*. At present such conduct can be prosecuted as public nuisance, though this is uncommon: one water authority informs us that it has never brought such a prosecution. The decision to prosecute Mr Goldstein was atypical, and is likely to have been influenced by the heightened public tension on the subject of anthrax attacks. Like the local authorities, public utilities generally prefer to use specialised offences: examples are interfering with the mail[5] (though this offence would not have applied to the particular facts of *Goldstein*) and with the sewerage[6] and water[7] networks. These offences, like public nuisance, are generally triable either in the Crown Court or in a magistrates' court: straightforward cases are dealt with in the magistrates' courts, the costs typically being between £1,000 and £2,000 according to the figures provided by one water authority, and generally being recoverable from the defence. In other instances, the utility companies bring civil actions, for example for negligence, nuisance or trespass.

Outraging public decency

According to the CPS, there are currently some 300-400 prosecutions for this offence each year. Many of these concern cases of indecent exposure: outraging public decency is used in preference to the statutory offence of exposure because the latter requires intention to alarm or distress.

POLICY OPTIONS

The following four policy options have been identified:

Option 1: Do nothing

The first option is to leave the current law as it stands. This would mean that the problems identified in the current law, outlined above under the heading 'Problems under Consideration', would remain.

Option 2: Alter the existing offences by statute

The second option would be to enact a statute providing that, to be guilty of either public nuisance or outraging public decency, the defendant must either have intended the adverse effects of his or her conduct, or been aware of the risk of those effects and nevertheless decided, without reasonable justification, to engage in that conduct.

Option 3: Abolish the existing offences and create new statutory offences

Policy option 3 would involve replacing the existing common law offences with two new statutory offences of public nuisance and outraging public decency. The aim would be to make the scope of the two offences the same as in option 2.

Regarding public nuisance, in the CP we present the argument that the codification of any common law offence is desirable in principle, and that public nuisance should not be an exception. We advise against using the conventional definition,

---

[5] Postal Services Act 2000 s 84.

[6] Water Industry Act 1991 ss 111,121.

[7] Water Industry Act 1991 s 174.

including the words "act not warranted by law or omission to fulfil a legal duty", and conclude that more work will need to be done on devising a suitable definition.

Regarding outraging public decency, policy option 3, restating the offence in statute, was not originally considered necessary. It is possible to remedy the specific problem identified under the current law, which is a narrow one, through targeted statutory provisions. Once more, however, codification is desirable in principle, and the detailed consideration of the ingredients of the offence, as presented in the CP, should provide the materials for a definition.

Option 4: Abolish the existing offences without replacement

Most cases which, under the current law, would be dealt with as public nuisance or as outraging public decency also fall under existing statutory schemes. For example, most nuisances could be dealt with as "statutory nuisances" under the Environmental Protection Act 1990 or else under the ASBO procedure, and many but not all cases of outraging public decency would fall within the offence of exposure under the Sexual Offences Act 2003. However, the two common law offences are considered more serious, and prosecuting authorities wish to keep the option of using them for cases of wilful or persistent behaviour.

OPTION APPRAISAL

Option 1: Do nothing

Costs

The cost of doing nothing is that of prosecuting and punishing those who create public nuisances or indecent displays without foresight of the consequences. These costs will fall on the courts, the prosecution, defendants and the legal aid fund.

A non-monetised cost is the perception among legal professionals and the public that the law is unfair and imposes a disproportionate sanction on what may be merely negligent or inadvertent conduct.

Benefits

The benefit of doing nothing is the avoidance of any immediate implementation costs.

Option 2: Alter the existing offences by statute

Costs

The main cost incidental to our proposals is that, while they exclude some cases from the scope of common law nuisance, procedures such as those for statutory nuisance will sometimes be brought instead. As mentioned below under "Benefits", we believe that these alternative procedures are usually cheaper than prosecution for nuisance and that there will be a net saving.

As we understand the position, both the CPS and the local authorities usually reserve common law public nuisance for cases of wilful misbehaviour for which the other procedures are inadequate; and these cases would not in any case be affected by our proposals. Accordingly the main effect of our proposals will be simply to confirm existing practice. The number of cases diverted from public nuisance to the other procedures is therefore likely to be small.

The same is normally true of nuisances affecting public utilities. The effect of our proposals will be that they can no longer prosecute in cases of negligent nuisance, such as was alleged by the prosecution in *Goldstein*. In some instances the effect will be that the individuals in question are not proceeded against at all; in others they may be prosecuted for specialised offences related to the utilities; in yet others civil proceedings will be brought. In the last case, this may result in a small increase in costs, as civil proceedings typically cost more than criminal. However, given the small number of public nuisance prosecutions at present brought by or on behalf of public utilities, this effect should be minimal.

There may be marginal cases in which time is spent on the issue of whether recklessness is present or not. This should not increase costs, as on the existing law there will equally be marginal cases (like *Goldstein*) where the issue is whether negligence is present or not.

We anticipate that the introduction of the new criterion of recklessness might be the subject of a small spike in appeals. Any costs that do arise in this context will be non-recurrent: once a disputed point has been settled the potential for appeal (and the costs associated with it) falls away. However, given the small overall number of prosecutions for the two offences, we expect these appeals to be rare.

There should be no effect on the costs to the Prison Service: public nuisance is an imprisonable offence, but the type of negligent behaviour affected by our proposals would never attract a prison sentence, whether it is prosecuted as a public nuisance or addressed through other procedures.

There will be minimal costs associated with publicising the changes to the law in this area. For the judiciary this would probably be achieved by inclusion in the monthly electronic newsletter circulated by the Judicial Studies Board, and by similar means within the prosecuting authorities and criminal defence services. There will also be some inevitable cost in money and Parliamentary time involved in introducing the legislation.

Benefits

We anticipate that there is likely to be a reduction in prosecutions for public nuisance as a result of the implementation of our recommendations, as merely negligent or inadvertent conduct will not be treated as an offence. In some cases this will lead to the use of alternative procedures. However, we believe that the cost of the alternative procedures will usually be less than that of prosecution for public nuisance (except possibly in some public utility cases), as most of the statutory offences are triable summarily only. The diversion of cases from public nuisance to the statutory offences should therefore result in a net saving. Figures for typical costs in the Crown Court and the magistrates' courts respectively, for offences comparable to public nuisance, are set out at the end of the section on "Key assumptions" below.

As concerns outraging decency, there will be some reduction in prosecutions for this offence, as prosecutions will not be brought (or if brought, will not succeed) in cases of inadvertent or purely negligent acts. It is unlikely that other proceedings will be brought in their place, as most of the alternative offences, e.g. exposure, also require intention. As with public nuisance, this should effect a saving in costs.

In the case of artistic displays, for example, our proposals will mean that prosecution will not succeed if there was no intention to cause offence or recklessness about the prospect of causing offence. By discouraging proceedings these cases, the new test should also lessen public perception that the law is enforcing outdated moral standards.

As a result of option 2 the law will be fairer and the criterion for criminal liability more appropriate. By targeting only wilful or reckless behaviour, the scope of the offences will be in keeping with their perceived gravity.

Option 3: Abolish the existing offences and create new statutory offences

Costs

The costs of option 3 would include all those mentioned under option 2, as both are ways of achieving what is basically the same reform in the law.

Since option 3 involves the complete restatement of the definitions of the offences there is some risk that for a short period following implementation there will be increased legal argument, longer trials and more appeals as a result of this proposal while the boundaries of the new offences are tested. The cost to HM Court Service of a day's hearing at the Crown Court is estimated at £5,690 and the cost of a day's hearing at the Court of Appeal is estimated at £14,415 (figures from 2007/8), with the parties' costs to be added on top in both cases. However, by careful drafting it should be possible to reduce this risk to a minimum.

Benefits

The benefit of reform under option 3 would include that of option 2, namely that the offences will be confined to wilful or reckless behaviour.

Codification of common law offences is always desirable in principle, as it demonstrates compliance with the human rights requirement of certainty and legality. It should also lead to reduced legal argument, shorter trials and fewer appeals in the medium to long term, as a fixed statutory definition will mean that there is less room to dispute either the legitimacy or the scope of the offence. A further benefit of codifying these offences now is that, should comprehensive codification of the criminal law be undertaken at a later stage, the work of codifying these two offences will already have been done and some time and effort will be saved at that later stage.

Cost/benefit analysis summary

Option 2 or 3 would provide necessary amendment and updating of the law at a proportionate cost. Of these, option 3 is the more comprehensive long-term solution.

KEY ASSUMPTIONS/RISKS

Key assumptions

Public nuisance broadly falls into two categories: environmental nuisance, enforced by local authorities, and behavioural nuisance, enforced by the police and Crown Prosecution Service. (Cases involving public utilities may be regarded as a third category, but with the exception of highway cases, which are dealt with by local authorities, these are uncommon.)

We are informed by local authorities that, in most cases of environmental nuisance, they prefer to use statutory procedures (e.g. enforcement notices under the Environmental Protection Act 1990), or else procedures under bye-laws. Further powers exist in housing cases, such as the condemnation of properties as unfit for habitation, or the repossession of premises from local authority tenants who have engaged in nuisance behaviour. We are further informed that prosecution for the common law offence of public nuisance is reserved for the most flagrant cases of wilful behaviour. We assume that this is correct and that, in relation to this category of cases, our proposed reform will simply reflect existing practice and therefore lead to no increase or reduction in prosecutions.

We are informed by the CPS that it brought 663 prosecutions for public nuisance between April 2007 and October 2009, representing an average of just over 250 cases a year. Following the case of *Rimmington*, which decided that series of acts against individuals, such as hate mail campaigns and obscene phone calls, do not fall within the offence, this figure is likely to fall, whether or not our proposed reform takes place. From the list of examples provided to us, it appears that the CPS also reserves this offence for wilful misbehaviour. The total number of prosecutions for this offence represents a tiny fraction of the total volume of "nuisance behaviour", as defined by the Home Office: there were 7,660[8] cases of "nuisance behaviour" reported on a day snap shot of crime in the UK. We assume that most of these cases are dealt with outside the criminal justice system, or by the ASBO procedure. We further assume that, as ASBOs are only made in response to wilful behaviour, our proposed reforms will have no knock-on effect in the form of an increase in the total number of ASBOs.

One category of cases which may be affected by our proposed reform is that of negligent acts which disrupt public access or services, as mentioned above under "Scale and context". As explained, the number of cases involved is minimal. Our key assumption in this area is that the information provided by the utility companies in our sample is representative of the practice of the utility companies generally.

---

[8]   Home Office Statistics, http://www.homeoffice.gov.uk/rds/pdfs04/dpr26.pdf.

We assume that the costs of public nuisance prosecutions are similar to those of criminal damage and public order offences. According to figures supplied by HM Court Service, typical costs of these cases (excluding prosecution and defence costs) are estimated as follows:

£11,000 per defendant in contested Crown Court cases

£1,500 per defendant in Crown Court cases in which there was an early plea of guilty

£1,600 per defendant in contested magistrates' court cases

£150-£300 per defendant in magistrates' court cases in which there was an early plea of guilty.

Risks

It is just possible that, if our proposals have the effect of reducing the number of prosecutions, this will encourage some private individuals to bring civil proceedings for the tort of public nuisance instead, with consequent civil legal aid costs on one or both sides. We regard this risk as minimal, as a person caused major loss by a public nuisance will wish to sue whether or not criminal proceedings are brought. In many cases a business responsible for a public nuisance will be a company rather than an individual, and therefore not eligible for civil legal aid,[9] while even in the case of individuals the scheme excludes allegations of personal injury or death (except through clinical negligence), damage to property and matters arising out of the carrying on of a business.[10]

It is also possible that, particularly in housing cases, the narrowing of public nuisance will spur local authorities into taking other proceedings, such as under landlord and tenant legislation or their statutory powers, or resort to mediation. This too is a small risk, as in most cases prosecution for public nuisance is a last resort after other remedies have been tried and proved ineffective. Many of the other remedies are also likely to be cheaper than prosecution for public nuisance.

There is a risk that the proposed recklessness test, and in the case of option 3 the general definition of the offence, will for a short period lead to failed prosecutions in marginal cases and an increase in appeals while the boundaries are tested. There is also the risk that too many defendants will claim the benefit of that test, possibly resulting in more lengthy trials. This effect may not be very significant, as the meaning of "recklessness" in other offences such as criminal damage is well established.

---

[9] Access to Justice Act 1999 s 4(1).

[10] Access to Justice Act 1999 Schedule 2 para 1.

SPECIFIC IMPACT TESTS

Legal Aid: It is anticipated that the proposals have the potential to generate a reduction in prosecutions, balanced by a slight increase in civil or administrative procedures and a small spike in appeals. This would result in a lightening of the burden of criminal legal aid, with a possible increase in the burden of civil legal aid. This increase is expected to be minimal or non-existent.

Race equality: Both the proposals and the existing offences appear to be ethnically neutral. Both offences concern the likely effect of certain activities on the public: activities with an effect on a special public, such as a local or ethnic community, are included.

Disability equality: The proposals have a positive impact, as by requiring a more conscious degree of intention they make it less likely that the offences will be committed inadvertently by people with cognitive disabilities.

Gender equality: Both the proposals and the existing offences appear to be neutral on gender as such. We have considered whether the existing offence of outraging public decency (and therefore any new offence with the same conduct element) may be discriminatory as to sexual orientation, for example whether activities by particular groups are more likely to cause public outrage. We believe that this risk is minimised by the requirement that the act must be such as to cause outrage to a reasonable person.

Human rights: The proposals have a positive human rights impact, as the offences will provide clearer guidance on the types of behaviour to be avoided. This meets the doubts that have been expressed, e.g. by the criminal law textbook Smith and Hogan, on whether the offence of outraging public decency in particular is certain enough to meet the requirements of Article 10 of the European Convention on Human Rights.

Specific Impact Tests: Checklist

Use the table below to demonstrate how broadly you have considered the potential impacts of your policy options.

Ensure that the results of any tests that impact on the cost-benefit analysis are contained within the main evidence base; other results may be annexed.

Type of testing undertaken	Results in Evidence Base?	Results annexed?
Competition Assessment	No	No
Small Firms Impact Test	No	No
Legal Aid	Yes	No
Sustainable Development	No	No
Carbon Assessment	No	No
Other Environment	No	No
Health Impact Assessment	No	No
Race Equality	Yes	No
Disability Equality	Yes	No
Gender Equality	Yes	No
Human Rights	Yes	No
Rural Proofing	No	No